THE LOST LETTERS OF JENNY LIND

THE LOST LETTERS
OF JENNY LIND

translated from the German

and edited with commentaries

by

W. Porter Ware and Thaddeus C. Lockard, Jr.

LONDON
VICTOR GOLLANCZ LTD
1966

MADE AND PRINTED IN GREAT BRITAIN BY
THE GARDEN CITY PRESS LIMITED
LETCHWORTH, HERTFORDSHIRE

ACKNOWLEDGMENTS

Although the nature of the letters translated in this book does not call for the same thorough-going investigation of all documents relating to the life of Jenny Lind which a biography would require, still we have attempted to search through most of the available material relating to her career. Our main aim has been to discover any details which might elucidate these German letters to Frau Wichmann. In the attainment of this aim, we have received aid from a number of people and guidance from several basic volumes on the subject, and we should like to acknowledge this assistance here.

We express our gratitude to Mr. Irving Lowens of the Music Division of the Library of Congress, Washington, D.C., who very kindly provided us with a photostat of Jenny Lind's letter in German addressed to the father of her future husband. This letter is quoted on pages 85-86.

Thanks also are due to Mr. James J. Heslin, Director of the New York Historical Society, and to his Assistant Museum Curator, Miss Carolyn Scoon, for permission to make a thorough study of the famous Leonidas Westervelt collection of Lindiana and also for permission to print their copy made from the original of Jenny Lind's letter to Dr. Baird of New York. (The whereabouts of this manuscript letter is now unknown, although about forty years ago it was in the possession of a lady in New York City.) It is printed on pages 87-88.

Mr. Samuel Pearce of The Museum of the City of New York, which houses the extensive Hildebrand collection of Lindiana, allowed us to make a careful study of these documents and memorabilia, although we were unable to make direct use of this material.

From among the many books concerning Jenny Lind which we have consulted, we should like to express our special indebtedness to the following :

Memoir of Madame Jenny Lind-Goldschmidt by Henry Scott Holland and W. S. Rockstro (John Murray, London, 1891).

The Life of Jenny Lind by her daughter, Mrs. Raymond Maude, O.B.E. (Cassell & Co. Ltd., London, 1926).

Jenny Lind: A Biography by Joan Bulman (James Barrie, London, 1956).

Jenny Lind, The Swedish Nightingale by Gladys Denny Schultz (J. B. Lippincott Co., New York, 1962).

Struggles and Triumphs, or Forty Years' Recollections of P. T. Barnum (The Courier Company, Buffalo, New York, 1875).

We should also like to express our particular gratitude to Jenny Lind's great-granddaughters—to Lady Welby, for so kindly allowing us to reproduce the photograph which faces page 96, and to Mrs. Oliver Woods for her friendly interest and help.

Finally, we are most of all indebted to Mrs. Sheila Bush, whose wide knowledge of the subject and deep insight into the problems involved in seeing the book through the press have proved to be invaluable.

CONTENTS

INTRODUCTION   9

PART I   19

PART II   89

APPENDIX   157

LIST OF ILLUSTRATIONS

Baxter print of Jenny Lind   *facing page* 32

Jenny Lind at Exeter Hall: bronze figure on marble   33

La Figlia del Reggimento: representation in metal and cloth   64

Worcester candle snuffer (1848) known as "Diffidence", showing Jenny Lind as the Swedish Nightingale   64

Cartoon in the *Illustrated London News* showing the fate of one enthusiast at Her Majesty's Theatre on the night of Jenny Lind's London début   65

This photograph was probably taken during one of Jenny Lind's early visits to London. Reproduced by kind permission of Lady Welby   96

View at Exeter Hall (*Illustrated London News*)   97

Facsimile of letter to Thackeray's daughter, enclosing tinted print of the writer   128

"Jenny Lind in some of her most celebrated characters" (*Illustrated London News* of November 12th 1887, ten days after her death)   129

INTRODUCTION

§ I

ALTHOUGH JENNY LIND is by now almost a legendary figure, and although her memory has been kept alive to the present day, little in the way of new material has turned up in this century to add to what was already known about her. The basic publication bearing on her life was a biography in two volumes prepared seventy-five years ago by two Englishmen, Henry Scott Holland and W. S. Rockstro, in collaboration with her husband, Otto Goldschmidt.[1] This work, plus research in the Westervelt collection of Lindiana (amassed over a long period of time by Leonidas Westervelt, and now owned by the New York Historical Society), has furnished most of the basic information for subsequent biographers, except for old magazine articles found here and there over the years. It is true that a little volume was published in 1926 by Jenny Lind's daughter, Jenny Maude,[2] which followed the Goldschmidts through their married years; yet the information contained therein might have been supplied by an outsider, and was almost entirely from known sources. Jenny Maude, in all probability, could have presented many intimate family details from her early life spent with her mother and father, but no doubt she was prevented from doing so by the typical Victorian reticence of a daughter discussing her parents' life together. The book itself seems quite formal. The

[1] *Memoir of Madame Jenny Lind-Goldschmidt: Her Early Art-Life and Dramatic Career, 1820–1851.* From original documents, letters, Ms. Diaries, etc., collected by Mr. Otto Goldschmidt. Prepared by Henry Scott Holland, M.A., Canon and Precentor of St Paul's, and W. S. Rockstro, author of "A General History of Music", "Life of Handel", "Life of Mendelssohn", etc. London: John Murray, 1891. In future references to this publication its title will be shortened to "Holland and Rockstro".

[2] *The Life of Jenny Lind* by Mrs. Raymond Maude, O.B.E., Cassell & Company Ltd., London.

interesting life by Joan Bulman which was published in 1956[3] contained a good deal of material from Swedish sources, and was given a particular appeal because the author had access to Otto Goldschmidt's diaries. Unfortunately the latter document is on the whole extremely dull, being filled with details about finance and similar matters.

Even in the two volumes of Holland and Rockstro the authors handled with gloves, or passed over entirely, the intimate details of the singer's life, though this was a very beautiful thing, without the slightest trace of scandal. Moreover, their story stopped in 1852, the last year of her American tour, for on February 5 of that year she married Otto Goldschmidt in Boston, and he felt that a curtain should be drawn thereafter. Here was something entirely too private to present to the world. And their host of friends in many countries might have taken offence at the printing of letters discussing their private affairs and mentioning names.

Otto Goldschmidt had a wealth of material in his hands—letters, documents, prints and mementoes. Here was the one great chance to reveal each step of Jenny's life in all its glowing, intimate details. Children and grandchildren of their friends had placed at his disposal collections of letters which Jenny had written over the years; yet only a fraction of this wealth of information was ever used. He chose not to step upon the toes of valued friends and neighbours, for much of this source material must have contained interesting private information which his discretion forbade him to use.

After a while this material was returned to the owners, the Goldschmidts retaining a portion of it. With the death of Otto Goldschmidt in 1907 there perished the greatest living memory of his wife's life.

Among the important material which Otto Goldschmidt must have seen and then returned to the Wichmann family in Berlin was undoubtedly the series of letters in German to Amalia Wichmann, spanning the years from 1845 to shortly before Amalia's death in 1876. Some of these letters were quoted in Holland and Rockstro, but often in an abbreviated form, and only up to the year of Jenny Lind's marriage in 1852, as men-

[3] *Jenny Lind: A Biography* by Joan Bulman, James Barrie, London.

tioned above. In this present volume, for the first time, they
are presented in full. They are addressed almost entirely to
Amalia Wichmann, with whom Jenny Lind invariably stayed
when she was in Berlin, and whose family she virtually adopted
as her very own, though a few of them are written to one or
other of the Wichmanns' sons. These letters, which recently
turned up in England and are now in our possession, have been
translated from the German, painstakingly, only during the past
few months, by the present editors. They furnish new information on Jenny's own opinion of her abilities as a singer and artist,
on her close union with her husband in marriage, on the years
they spent together giving concerts in Europe, and on their retirement in England.

§ 2

Let us consider for a moment the linguistic characteristics of
these German letters. Jenny Lind undoubtedly possessed an in-
born talent for languages, and the many grammatical similarities
between her native Swedish and German must have given her
a head-start in the latter language. She did not begin the
systematic study of German, however, until after her twenty-
fourth year. In 1844-45 she studied German intensively in Berlin with Madame Birch-Pfeiffer, a literary figure with a considerable reputation there, and soon her style in German became
consistently excellent. Even her "errors" in German could be
termed indigenous, the kind that cultivated native Germans
also make when they hastily scribble informal letters to their
close friends.

Jenny's handwriting is very personal and idiosyncratic : rather
small and regular in the earlier letters, but growing increasingly
bolder and freer with the passage of the years. Hers was always
a flowing line, almost as if her innate lyricism were expressing
itself visibly in the ink that came from her pen. We possess one
letter of hers in the traditional German script still in use in the
nineteenth century, but all the other letters were written in stan-
dard modern European handwriting. Contrary to the accepted
usage in German of capitalizing all nouns, Jenny frequently
wrote her nouns with small initial letters, and sometimes did

likewise even for the beginning words of sentences. This, plus her private system of punctuation and paragraphing, all conspire to give her letters to Amalia Wichmann a stamp of individuality.

She could, of course, whenever formal occasions demanded it, write flawless ceremonial German prose, and she could do the same in French and English too. But in these letters to the woman whom she perhaps admired and loved most, her style quickly became, and remained, the spontaneous overflow of a warm and loving heart. As early as May, 1846, Felix Mendelssohn had written to her: "You write so well! In fact, when I get a letter from you, it is exactly as if I saw you or heard you speak. I can see the expression of your face at every word that stands written before me . . ."[4]

Not only do we get in these letters the basic external facts of the singer's busy life, but we are also given what is much more important: an intimate revelation of her feelings, disappointments and hopes. Through them all runs an astounding modesty: never once does she praise herself, and she quotes the praise of others rarely, and then only with self-deprecatory irony or humorous disapproval. Humour pervades many of her remarks; but even stronger is her sense of the sadness in life and the tragedy that faces every living being. Behind everything, however, lies her deep religious faith and her sense of dedication, her humble acceptance of her great gift, and her determination to use her talent for the glory of God and the edification—and aid—of others. These letters to her best friend—a person severely tried by chronic illness and numerous family problems—are strewn with religious admonitions and philosophical exhortations. If these expressions were isolated and catalogued, many of them would turn out to be conventional clichés of the period, but, read within their context in the warm flow of Jenny's written line, they reveal the wonderful understanding and empathy which she felt for her correspondent.

If the ethical content of these letters could be epitomized in one word, that word might well be "loyalty". From the very first letter to Amalia Wichmann through almost thirty years of correspondence, terminated only by Amalia's death, there runs

4 *Maude*, p. 67.

the unbroken thread of faithfulness and gratitude. To modern
ears, perhaps, much of the terminology of these letters, and
especially the phrases of endearment used at their close, will
sound exaggerated and even false. Nothing could be further
from the actual fact, as the percipient reader will realize when
he understands the true nature of these letters, written to the
person whom Jenny called "my honoured *mother, sister, friend*".
(See letter of November 4, 1866.) These phrases are not com-
plimentary in the traditional sense of the word; she meant what
she wrote, and one of her concluding phrases, "from your true-
unto-death loving Jenny", was typical of her life as well as of
her letters.

§ 3

At this point it might be well to glance at Jenny Lind's life
prior to her friendship with the Wichmann family. This was far
from being a rosy path leading to certain success. Quite the
contrary : unhappy with her parents, living in straightened circumstances in other people's homes, working ceaselessly day and
night, undergoing setbacks and disappointments, struggling to
overcome her innate shyness—the young Jenny had to fight
every step of her way. It was lucky for her that, together with
her voice, God had endowed her with another great gift : an
unswerving faith in her mission as a singer.

She was born in Stockholm on October 6, 1820, and was
baptized Johanna Maria Lind. Her father, Niclas Jonas Lind,
the son of a lace manufacturer, was both young—he was twenty-
two—and immature for the responsibilities he had to shoulder.
Her mother, of respectable burgher stock, had made an unhappy
marriage in 1810, at the age of 18, to a Captain Radberg. This
had terminated in divorce.

At the time of Jenny's birth, her mother was engaged in
running a day school for girls. Jenny's grandmother, Fru Teng-
mark, was the first to detect the child's musical talents, for the
grandmother seemed to have a deeper attachment to the little
girl than did the parents themselves.

By the time Jenny had reached her ninth year, her depth
of feeling and her precociousness were predominant in her

personality. Mlle. Lundberg, an artist who had heard her sing, was so impressed with the voice that she attempted to awaken in the parents an appreciation of such God-given talent. Mlle. Lundberg passed on her discovery to Herr Croelius, a music-master well known in Stockholm. He, in turn, introduced her to Count Puke, the head of the Swedish Royal Theatre, who was astonished at the unlikely appearance of the little girl. It was only after much persuasion by Herr Croelius that the Count consented to an audition, but the golden voice with its heart-searching quality won him over completely. He decided there-upon that she should immediately be enrolled in the *Ecole Musicale,* which was attached to the Theatre Royal of Stock-holm.

Jenny owed much of her early musical training, also, to the Court singer Isak Berg, and to the Swedish composer Lindblad, from whom she learned to appreciate Swedish melody.

Her first appearance on the stage took place during these musical studies, when she played children's parts in dramatic pieces. But at the age of thirteen her voice weakened, and for a while her hopes of becoming a finished singer were dimmed. Nevertheless, she continued with her studies four years more, in the modest hope of becoming a singing teacher. Life was hard for Jenny, whose parents were utterly unsympathetic to her both as a daughter and as a budding artist. The main interest they took in her singing was due to their desire to exploit it financially for their own profit.

It is impossible to imagine what sufferings and indignities Jenny must have experienced before making up her mind to live independently of her parents. But this she did as soon as she was legally of age. The deprivation during her earlier years of any-thing like motherly love may explain the readiness with which she responded later to Amalia Wichmann's maternal feelings in Berlin. For Amalia, the mother of three sons, who still longed for a daughter, Jenny Lind seemed predestined to fill this vacant spot to perfection.

At this period of her life, it happened that a concert was to be given in the Theatre Royal in Stockholm. It was planned to present Act Four of *Roberto il Diavolo,* but there was no one capable of singing the role of Alice. When Jenny was tried out in the part, it was found to the astonishment of all that her voice was better than ever before. In fact, she was so well received in the performance that the audience considered her already to be a young *prima donna*.

The first real success came in her portrayal of Agatha in Weber's *Der Freischütz*, in 1838, and during the next two years she had much experience in the parts with which she was to become intimately identified later on, and in which she was to gain considerable fame.

By 1840 she was the idol of the national drama, and had received high official recognition by being appointed Court Singer. Nevertheless, there were already signs that her voice was deteriorating—perhaps because so many demands had been made on it while she was still so young—and she herself felt that there was something lacking in her training. This was why she sought out the well known singing teacher, Manuel Garcia, in Paris in July, 1841. Her main success in Sweden up to now had been due primarily to her histrionic ability and the natural qualities of her voice. Now came the chance, through rigid professional training, to realize the full potential of this great and unique instrument. Garcia gave her little encouragement at first, and asked her to wait for a period of at least three months. He felt that her voice had reached the breaking point, and that the only hope was a rest from any practice whatsoever. During the waiting period Jenny Lind studied French and Italian, and she mastered the art of reading music at sight.

Upon the completion of her training, which lasted for about a year, Jenny returned to Sweden, where she was warmly received. Soon she became the pride of Stockholm, and in the next six years she was extremely successful in Finland, Denmark, Germany and Austria.

During this time she still refused to live with her parents, and in compliance with Swedish law, which required an unmarried woman to have a legally appointed guardian, she obtained the services of Judge Henrik Munthe. This was one of the happiest choices of her life, for Judge Munthe turned out to be not only an efficient manager of her financial affairs, but also a warm and helpful friend. Their friendship continued throughout the years of her married life.

While Jenny Lind was in Paris, Meyerbeer had had the chance to hear her sing at a private audition. Since this audition had brought no offers in France, and since he recognized immediately the potentialities of her voice, Meyerbeer persuaded her to accept an engagement at the court theatre in Berlin, where she made her first appearance as *Norma* on December 15, 1844.

§ 4

Between the time of her arrival in Berlin and her performance at the opera, Jenny Lind had been introduced—probably by Meyerbeer—to a person who was to exert a greater influence upon her than any other human being, except for her husband. This person was Amalia Wichmann, the recipient of the letters of Jenny Lind which form the basis of this book.

These letters are presented chronologically, and fall naturally into two groups: letters in the first group were composed by "Jenny Maria Lind" prior to her marriage in 1852, while letters in the second group were written by "Jenny Lind-Goldschmidt" after her marriage. Part I of our book reproduces those letters most of which were partially used in Holland and Rockstro under the supervision of, and in close collaboration with, Otto Goldschmidt. In Part II are the letters which have never been translated or presented to the public in any form whatsoever.

We should explain that in Part I there will be found several letters to Amalia the originals of which are either destroyed or are at any rate not in our possession. On the other hand we possess, and present in this book, certain other letters of this earlier period which were not used even in part in the famous early biography. Most of the letters in Part I, therefore, are presented more fully in our volume than in Holland and Rockstro; for wherever our collection contains autograph letters which were quoted, often only in part, in Holland and Rockstro, we have carefully collated the English version given in that book with Jenny's original manuscript letters in German. From our original letters we have inserted the omitted words, the excluded phrases and the sentences dropped in that basic work. The

Holland and Rockstro translation is sometimes awkward, and frequently seems to be a literal, non-idiomatic translation from the original German. It is our conjecture that these parts were translated by Otto Goldschmidt himself, a native of Hamburg, and that Holland and Rockstro, who may not have seen the original letters at all, diplomatically accepted his abridged, literal translations just as they were. In general, we have kept to this version, but occasionally, for the sake of ease in reading, we have adopted a more colloquial rendering—while not, of course, altering in any way the sense or the spirit of the original. In the portions of our manuscript letters which Holland and Rockstro did not use, and of course in *all* the manuscript letters found in Part II, we have aimed at a more idiomatically English translation, while still attempting to maintain the spirit and tone of letters written in the latter half of the nineteenth century.

Wherever possible, we have identified in the linking passages or by footnotes the persons and happenings to which Jenny Lind refers. In some cases, naturally, this is impossible; but we hope that in the years to come researchers may stumble across the answers to some of the little riddles of this type that we cannot solve.

It is especially to the second part of this volume that the word "lost" in our title applies. Although these "lost" letters, thirty-nine in number, were probably seen by Otto Goldschmidt in 1888, after the publication of that book they disappeared from public view and have been inaccessible to the public until recently discovered by the editors of this volume.

We believe that our presentation of these letters is worthwhile; our search for Lind memorabilia in foreign countries, through byways of London and Paris, in Third and Second Avenue antique shops in New York City and in the archives in the cities of the United States where Jenny sang during her tour of 1850-52, has helped to create a broader, more intimate revelation of Jenny's life than the public has ever known before. However, this volume makes no attempt to take the place of any one of several splendid biographies published during the past hundred years. Rather, we urge the interested reader to avail himself of one or more of these books, placing them alongside our little volume. We trust that he will find our own a most desirable addition.

W. Porter Ware and Thaddeus Lockard

The University of the South,
Sewanee, Tennessee.

PART I

PART I

JENNY LIND'S GENIUS was formed by a combination of a very remarkable voice, unmatched, in our opinion, by any female singer in this century or the last one, and a born talent as an actress. Her forceful and beautiful character makes one who delves into the facts of her life feel that God must have sent her to earth as his special envoy and for a special purpose. Her generous gifts to the unfortunate throughout her life, her love of the pure and decent, her patience with those who could not hope to measure up to her greatness, set her apart as one of few such personalities in all history.

After her sojourn in Paris, her voice developed into a brilliant and powerful soprano, with varying shades and a lovely quality. Its compass extended from B below the line to G in the fourth line above it, a clear two and three-quarter octaves. The F sharp was so remarkable that Mendelssohn had it particularly in mind when he wrote for her "Hear ye, Israel".[5] Years later, her husband used the same famous note in the air in his oratorio *Ruth,* which was especially written for her. The upper A was given prominence in a syncopated passage of a cadence sung by Jenny Lind in *Casta Diva,* and in a favourite Swedish melody. According to the critics of her day, her pianissimo rendering of the high notes became a famous feature of her singing, for it reached every corner of the largest auditorium, although delivered in a whisper. The renewal of her breath was effected so artfully that no one, however close to her, could notice it. Apparently no singer of her day could rival the swelling or diminishing of her voice from the softest *piano* to the fullest power. The shakes, scales, legato and staccato passages brought astonishment and admiration from both music critics and the public in general.

Jenny first met the Wichmanns on October 21, 1844, when

[5] From *Elijah,* composed in 1846, soon after the Lower Rhine Festival at Aix-la-Chapelle.

she attended a soirée at their house in the Hasenheger Strasse. The introduction came about when Lady Westmorland, whose husband was at that time English Ambassador at the Court of Prussia and who was a close friend of Amalia Wichmann, met Jenny at a small musical party at the Princess of Prussia's (later the Empress Augusta), following Meyerbeer's desire to have persons of importance meet the new singer. It seemed to be a natural thing for Amalia Wichmann and her family to become fast friends with the lonely young singer, and over the years the friendship blossomed into the closest intimacy.

Professor Wichmann was a well known sculptor, and he and his wife attracted into their circle such people as Mendelssohn (whom Jenny met on that first visit at their home), Herr Taubert, the conductor and composer, Professor Edward Magnus, a painter of note, Professor Werder, Professor Schnackenberg, Graf von Schlieffen, Concertmeister Ries, and on rarer occasions Lenné (the landscape gardener and originator of the royal plantations around Potsdam), Graf von Redern (Director of the Court Music), and an assortment of distinguished artists, men of letters and intellectuals. Nor should we overlook such guests of the Wichmann *salon* as Herr Heinrich Brockhaus, head of the great publishing house of that name in Leipzig, a man of wide influence and culture.

The first known letter written by Jenny to Amalia Wichmann was dated about a year after this initial meeting with the family. It was in French, for Jenny was still too unsure of herself even to attempt a letter in German.[6]

I

Niedstädten bei Altona, October 28, 1845

Bien Chère et Aimable Madame Wichmann,

I am very grateful for the kind letter which I had the honour to receive from you, and more delighted still to find that you

---

[6] In the appendix we give the page references to Holland and Rockstro, and also indicate which sections of each letter in Part I are quoted in that book.

retain for me the kindly feeling which makes me so pleased and happy.

I have been unwell for some time. I caught cold at Copenhagen, and was therefore unable to go to Hanover or Bremen or anywhere else. Because of this indisposition I am now staying with a very good friend, Madame Arnemann, near the town of Altona, where I am getting quite well, and resting.

But in any event I must go to Berlin, and it is for this reason, dear Madame, that I take the liberty of informing you that I leave this place tomorrow morning—or on the 30th; and I expect to be in Berlin on the 31st.

I go from here to Zelle, and from thence I hope to reach Berlin, by railway, in a day. Today is Monday, and on Friday I hope to have the pleasure of seeing you again.

It will be very nice to have my maid there. I only feared, Madame, on your account, that it would not be agreeable to you to have so many strange faces about you. I hope to find you in good health, and your family also; until then goodbye, dear, good and kind Madame Wichmann.

I am

Your very grateful and devoted

Jenny Lind

This letter, with its traditional formality, forms a marked contrast to the intimate and devoted letters which Jenny was soon to write in German to Amalia. As Otto Goldschmidt commented in later years: "The young artist [his future wife] stood sorely in need of a trusty friend and counsellor, in whose good faith and loyalty she could place unbounded confidence, and upon whom she could lavish the wealth of affection with which her own true heart was overflowing. To an ardent and impulsive nature like hers the love of such a friend was priceless, and Madame Wichmann proved herself well worthy of the confidence she inspired. She was a woman of marked ability, unvarying discretion, amiable and prepossessing to the last degree, and beloved by all who knew her."

Amalia's husband was in his sixties at that time, and much her senior. He was a member of the Order of Knights of the Red Eagle, a friend of Thorwaldsen and the favourite pupil of

Schadow, both well-known sculptors. In Holland and Rockstro a quaint little sketch of the Wichmann living-room is shown, drawn by their son Otto. This memento was kept by Jenny and treasured over the years. At her death it was found with the inscription : "A room in Professor Wichmann's house in Berlin, where we oft were sitting till late in the night conversing with Mendelssohn and Taubert."

Jenny's next letter to Amalia is written three months later :

II

Weimar, January 27, 1846

Älskade Fru [Dearest lady] :

Yes ! if I might only continue in my mother-tongue—then my dearest Frau Professorin would have the chance of receiving a fairly nice letter. But, in German ! Ah !

Weimar is only a little place, but it is very interesting. However, I will not tell you about it now, but will wait until I get to Berlin.

I stay here until Thursday morning, January 29, when I go to Erfurt, to sing at a concert there. From thence I go, on Friday, to Leipzig, where I stay for the night; and you will understand, gracious Professorin, the source of my kind invitation : can you not guess? and on Saturday we come, by the first train, to Berlin.

Your grateful and sincerely devoted,

Jenny Lind

The invitation mentioned above was one given to her by Felix and Cécile Mendelssohn. Mrs. Mendelssohn was the former Cécile Jeanrenaud, whose French family had settled in Frankfurt. The Mendelssohn family, with its devotion and warmth, had accepted Jenny as their close friend. The two great musicians were each an inspiration to the other, but their association lasted for only a short time because of Mendelssohn's untimely death in 1847, while still in his thirties.

Jenny left Berlin, after the last engagement, on April 2nd,

taking with her her faithful companion Mlle. Louise Johansson,
a girlhood friend, for engagements in Vienna, pausing at Leipzig to spend a few days as the guest of the Heinrich Brockhauses. These two were very fond of her, and Herr Brockhaus
commented, "It is impossible not to like the girl from the very
bottom of one's heart. She has such a noble and beautiful
nature."

Jenny's good friend, Madame Arnemann, was passing through
Leipzig about this time, and Jenny left the Brockhauses' in order
to be with her. While still at the Brockhauses', she wrote to
Amalia as follows:

III

Leipzig, April 1846 [Believed to be April 8th or 9th]
Dearly Beloved Amalia:

If I could only tell you everything that I am feeling at this
moment! If I could only send you an impression of my heart
so that you could see why it is full to overflowing!

I am quite sure that you understand me, and you know that
I shall love you always and eternally. You will certainly believe,
too, that this is not just a polite phrase, but expresses the true
sentiments of my grateful heart.

God bless you all, and give you, some day, tenfold the good
that you have given me! For, Amalia, for the first time in my
life I have felt as if I had tasted the blessedness of home.

What more can I say? All the rest, you can imagine for
yourself. I will only tell you this—that, if I did not have the
prospect of seeing you again soon, it would go very sadly indeed with me; for my heart now clings to you so that nothing
else can satisfy me.

It was really good of you, Amalia, to write to me straight
away, and I thank you. It put my mind quite at ease.

In Bernburg everything was terribly dismal and I was happy
when I came here yesterday evening. I went to the Mendels-
sohns' immediately, and the friendliness I was shown there
helped me a great deal. And I could talk about all of you. I

am staying with the Brockhauses, and they are so kind and friendly.

But above all I miss my children,[7] my poor professor and my *älskade*. But it is real happiness, in fact the greatest happiness, to feel so deep—I should like to say so inexhaustible—a love as that which I feel for all of you. God protect you. I am expecting Mathilda Arnemann, and I will write to you once more from here, dearest friend. You know how happy a few lines will make me. So write me a few words without delay, and tell me everything you would like me to know.

And you need not be afraid that they will not be well received. Farewell. What you mean to me I cannot say. I am only thankful to my Creator, who gave me so deep a feeling.

Does Amalia understand that I love her as much as her own children do, and is she aware that for this life, and even beyond, I shall always call myself *her*

Jenny

P.S. Our good Louise talks about you all the time. Yet you have *never* referred to *her*. She sends her greetings ! ! !

On April 12 Jenny and Mendelssohn gave a concert at the Leipzig Gewandhaus, where Mendelssohn was at that time conducting. These concerts were regarded as being the finest to be heard anywhere in Europe. During the performance an added attraction was the unexpected arrival of Madame Clara Schumann (née Wieck), whom Mendelssohn escorted from the audience to join them on the stage, when, still in her travelling dress, she played two of his *Songs Without Words*.

Jenny left Leipzig with her friend Madame Arnemann on April 13 and proceeded to Carlsbad, remaining there until the sixteenth. Then, with her companion Louise Johansson, she continued her journey to Vienna, arriving on Saturday, April 18. She stayed there at the home of Dr. Vivanot, a physician of note, whose residence stood in one of the principal thoroughfares, Am Graben.

She had been engaged to sing at the Theater an der Wien,

[7] Jenny Lind is referring to the Wichmann sons. They were, in order of birth, Herrmann, Rudolph, and Otto.

the first performance being *Norma* on April 22, 1846. When she first saw the theatre, at that time the biggest in Vienna, she was appalled by its size, and could only with great difficulty be persuaded to carry on with the rehearsal. Although her performances were greeted with tremendous ovation—the crowds were greater, and the prices higher, than at any time within living memory—she was not as happy as she had been in Berlin, as the following letter shows.

IV

Wien, April 27, 1846

My dearest :

I should have written to you a long time before now, but these days have been so hectic that I have had to remain silent until now. I sent a few lines to Birch-Pfeiffer,[8] of course, but that is a commitment which I had made a solemn promise to fulfil.

How blissfully happy your letter made me! A thousand thanks, beloved, sweet Amalia. Oh! I think of you all so often, and it always seems to me so extremely strange that I must live separated from all of you—sometimes things just don't make sense. But what a number of difficult things one must bear in life!

I have been suffering from home-sickness again; and, though I may justly say that I am at home everywhere, I really feel quite homeless. Do you understand me, Amalia? That is how it is with me : it is so. It was only when I lived with you that I had no such longings.

[8] Under her maiden name, Charlotte Pfeiffer had appeared on the stage with success in Munich, Vienna, Berlin and other important cities. In middle age she retired from the stage, marrying Dr. Christian Birch of Copenhagen, son of a Danish Minister of State. Thereafter she devoted herself to dramatic authorship, producing nearly seventy plays, among them *Die Marquise von Villette* and *Die Frau Professorin*. Jenny, who was always extremely meticulous about her libretti, consulted her often, and found her advice on German renderings of great value. She died on August 25, 1868, four days before her husband.

So far everything has gone splendidly here. I have appeared twice in *Norma;* and was called so many times before the curtain that I was quite exhausted. Bah! I don't like it. Everything should be done in moderation; otherwise it is not pleasing.

I haven't been here long enough to be able to give a real judgment, but this much I can assure you, that I like the Berlin public *ten thousand times* better. You simply can't imagine the things that please the public here. I was recently in an opera and I came home indignant! The so-called leading lady is Fräulein Marra, who sings and acts in such a way that Fräulein Marx would appear a heavenly divine figure by comparison. Oh, good heavens![9]

And so you mustn't imagine that it is possible to find in Vienna a beloved person like yourself or my professor, or like my "children", or that one meets such people as Professor Werder, Taubert, and the like. Nothing of the sort, dearest Amalia! I stick to my guns. I have found all of you, and now I can thank my Maker for it on my knees. You are all I need. I spend many wakeful hours at night, and now I am looking forward to my trip back. It is a lucky thing when one has a stout heart, but sometimes it is difficult.

How glad I should be, if Taubert were really to come here. I dare not build too much upon it; but it would be very pleasant.

Yesterday I had a letter from Mme. Arnemann. She asked whether we would like to do the "Schmentzer" [?] aria in the opera [illegible] at her house. She is still ill and is suffering excruciating pain.

May I ask you to greet Graf von Redern once more for us when you see him, and tell him that I am getting along quite satisfactorily?

I should like to write another page, but I write so badly, and besides my heart is so full when I think of you that I just can't find the right words. Therefore, farewell. I will write to all of you again soon.

[9] Jenny Lind's distress was justified, for the cast, with two exceptions, was exceedingly poor: of the tenor, the *Wiener Musik-Zeitung* wrote that "he sang no worse than usual".

You all know what you mean to me, and this feeling will endure forever.

Thine,

Jenny

P.S. How much pleasure my bird has given me, which Rudolf sent. How beautifully I have written this page, Herrmann![10]

Nine days went by, and Jenny wrote once again. The letter was obviously scribbled in haste, and seems to indicate great emotion at the time of writing.

V

Vienna, May 6, 1846

Dearest :

It gives me as much pleasure as pain to learn that you have been longing to receive a few more lines from me. I knew, of course, that you were fond of me and that [now] you love me, but I had no idea of the extent of your affection! Beloved, dear Amalia! How can I thank you? And how can I find words in which to express my feelings? If I had thought that you were anxious, I should have written to you much more often. Only I have always felt that everything was [illegible] between us, and everything concerning us was so unshakeably sure and as it should be—indeed, *exactly* as it must be, when a heartfelt lasting love exists between persons—that it is not important whether we write to each other often or seldom. And it never entered my head that for this reason you could imagine me to be indifferent. Because you know too how deeply I feel for you and how much I love you; for this great gift is not only granted for the present, but is given for one's whole life and on into eternity.

I think of you, daily and hourly; and it has gone badly with me since I parted from you, my beloved friends.

I have been so homesick that I scarcely knew whether I should

[10] Jenny Lind refers humorously to ink blots towards the top centre of the inside pages, and calls further attention to these blots by writing "Herrmann" beside them.

live or die; and so frightfully melancholy, and sad, that it is a long time since I have felt anything like it. Do you understand me? I never felt this anguish while I was with you.

It never occurred to me to feel lonely then. Truly, I have not written to you about it much, for if I did you would be reading nothing but Jeremiads from me. But didn't you receive a letter from me here in Vienna?

But I am better now; and the day before yesterday Taubert came. Ah, what a joyful surprise!—what memories of the past winter!—it all shines so brightly before me now!

And now I must tell you a little about the Theatre, and things of that sort.

Dearest, dearest lady![11]

Do you know, I have been placed in the very worst and most unfavourable circumstances; and yet, I have never had a greater triumph! Just think of this!

To begin with; Herr Pokorny[12] actually had the rashness to demand such frightful prices that a single reserved seat cost eight gulden, and a box forty! Such prices have been unheard of since the time of Catalani,[13] and the public were furious about it.

Secondly; with these high prices, Pokorny engaged for the first ten performances a tenor whom everyone laughed at. Everything depended upon me; I was made the sacrifice. And all this I had to bear and do penance for.

Thirdly, the whole Italian faction was opposed to me, and was determined to hiss if there was the slightest thing that could be found fault with.

And now a circumstance which was so terribly ridiculed before I came on, that is, on the steps in *Norma,* which was not very encouraging either! Nevertheless, everything has gone well; and my success is only so much the greater, and I almost believe

----

[11] In the original letter, these three words are written "Älskade, älskade Fru!" and underlined three times.

[12] The manager of the Theater an der Wien.

[13] The famous Italian singer, who made her début at Venice in 1795. From that moment she became the rage, sought after by every impresario in Europe. For nearly thirty years she sang in most of the great opera houses, spending seven years in England as the leading *prima donna.*

that the good Lord did this on purpose to teach me, gently, that when one serves *Him* and only loves [illegible], then the opposition of the whole world can accomplish nothing.

With divine weapons all evil is literally dashed to the ground. Even *those Italians!*

Taubert is sitting with me now and playing to me; and I persuade myself that I am with you, living in quietness and peace, and am assured that you all know with what deep and true love I cling to you, and how impossible it would be for me ever to love you less.

The letter breaks off here at the foot of the page, for, as Otto Goldschmidt found out long ago, the final portion was cut off. The mutilation also destroyed some of the text on the reverse side of the sheet. An added note in the margin suffered in the deletion, a remark about Professor Wichmann. Along the edge of the first page of the letter she has added : "Louise sends her regards and thanks you from the bottom of her heart for your letter."

There had been opposition to Jenny's singing in Vienna by three rival *prime donne* : Mesdames Stoeckel-Heinefetter and Hasselt-Barth and Fräulein Anna Zerr. In spite of this, Jenny created a profound impression in Bellini's *La Sonnambula* as well as in his *Norma,* rendering the title roles of these operas with such sensitive feeling and superb acting that it quite melted the hearts of all who saw and heard her.

The organizers of the Lower Rhine Musical Festival had been in touch with Jenny Lind since very early in the year 1846, in the hope of securing her presence at the twenty-eighth meeting of the Association, to take place at Aix-la-Chapelle (Aachen) on the 31st of May and the 1st and 2nd of June. Consequently, she left Vienna on May 23rd to meet Mendelssohn at Frankfurt on the evening of the 26th, so that they might go together to Aix-la-Chapelle. Accompanied by Mlle. Louise Johansson, they started down the Rhine on Wednesday, the 27th, by steamboat. In Aix Jenny was the guest of the Marquis and Marquise de Sassenay, while Mendelssohn stayed at the hotel *Grand Monarque.* The festival, which included arias from *The Crea-*

tion and *Alexander's Feast* and songs by Mendelssohn, was sensationally successful. It was generally regarded as being the best within living memory, largely owing to Jenny Lind's own radiance and the inspiration which she gave to the other performers.

Jenny's affection for the Wichmann sons shows itself in a letter which she sent to their second son at this time :

VI

Aachen, June 2, 1846

My dear Rudolph :

My pleasure in Aachen will soon come to an end, for all will be over today, and early tomorrow we leave. But I believe Mendelssohn means to accompany us a little way, and we hope to see the view from the Drachenfels, which will be very nice.

How well everything went with me in Vienna! Only my manservant was very nearly crushed to death, owing to the enthusiasm, so that I had to leave him behind in Frankfurt, and he has only just now rejoined me.

Farewell, my dear boy. Greetings from

Your Sister

Felix Mendelssohn and Jenny Lind did, indeed, enjoy the trip farther down the Rhine. As well as seeing the Drachenfels they spent an afternoon at Königswinter and a pleasant day at Cologne, after which she proceeded to Hanover, where she was engaged for performances at the Court Theatre.

Leaving Hanover, Jenny went on to Hamburg to fill an engagement for a series of twelve guest performances at the Stadt Theater, giving in addition two benefit performances. She stayed in the home of her friends the Arnemanns at Nienstädten, near Altona. The Arnemann family also invited Mina Fundin, an old friend of Jenny's from Stockholm, to keep her company.

The Arnemanns pressed Mendelssohn to visit them at this time, hoping that he would stay on his way to England, as soon as he had completed his *Elijah,* which was to be presented at Birmingham. But the last portion of the oratorio proved to be so taxing on his strength that he felt unable to accept, much to his sorrow.

Baxter print of Jenny Lind

Jenny Lind at Exeter Hall: bronze figure on marble

Jenny began her second season at Hamburg on June 22, giving her favourite opera *Norma*, followed by *La Sonnambula*, *Don Juan*, *Lucia di Lammermoor* and, finally, *La Figlia del Reggimento* (this last one for the first time in Germany).

The Wichmanns—Amalia and two of her sons—spent four days in Hanover with Jenny, during which time they tried to persuade her to take a trip with them to Switzerland at the close of summer, hoping that Mendelssohn also would join them. A letter from Jenny which followed some time later expresses her feeling that she had been working beyond her strength and needed absolute rest.

VII

Nienstädten, July 4, 1846

Dear Amalia!

Beloved Amalia! I feel quite exhausted. After all, these fatigues leave their mark, and convince me that I am not strong enough to undertake such a journey without injury to my health. I must sing here a few times more—but that cannot be helped. I have consulted a physician; for these nervous contractions from which I am suffering rendered it indispensable. He says it is absolutely necessary that I should go somewhere to take the baths. My nerves, he says, are in a very bad condition; and I ought to have done it long ago. I know the doctors in Sweden recommended this four years ago; but I could not possibly do it then.

I have quite made up my mind that next summer, or next autumn at the latest, I will leave the stage. I will, therefore, make the best use I can of the time; and as I have already arranged for the coming season it is only sensible, now, to husband my strength for next winter.

Greet my beloved there, from your ever loving

Jenny

Jenny Lind's deep rooted conviction that the operatic stage

was not the ideal life for her crops up many times in biographies of her life. She had a strong desire to leave opera for oratorio or concert singing. She mentions this determination in letters not only to Mme. Wichmann but also to her guardian, Judge Munthe, Mme. Birch-Pfeiffer, Mrs. Grote,[14] and others.

VIII

Nienstädten, August 1, 1846

Dearly Beloved Amalia!

Today, I sing for the poor; and positively for the last time [on the operatic stage].

On Thursday, the fourth of August, I go to Cuxhaven, with the Brunton family. (Do you remember the long letters that the daughter, Fräulein von Seminoff, used to write to me?) They have always been very kind to me. There I shall be able to rest and take the sea baths for four weeks.

In the meantime Louise stays here, to take care of her health; for she is ordered to drink the mineral waters. When I have done with Cuxhaven, I shall come here again; for I am very happy here, and I can only compare this family with yours.

I shall rest until about September 20. Then I go, first to Frankfurt; thence to Munich, as you know; and from Munich to Stuttgart—but this will be later on. From Stuttgart, I go to Vienna.

When shall I see you again? If we could only go to Paris together, next summer, somewhere about the month of June! I should so much like to see Garcia again before I leave Germany for ever.

---

[14] Mrs. Grote's family, including Madame von Koch, her sister, had been close to Jenny Lind in the early years at Stockholm. Mrs. Grote married a well-known historian of Ancient Greece. She had busied herself for some years in preparing a life of Jenny Lind but at her death this was only partly completed. The memoir terminated with the year 1848. It contained sixty closely written pages which Otto Goldschmidt saw after the death of his wife. Frequent quotations from Mrs. Grote's diary are given in Holland and Rockstro.

God keep you! Write to me again soon, and I will duly
answer you. Ah, Amalia! next spring I shall be free! I am
afraid so great a happiness will never fall to my lot.

Your ever truly loving

Jenny

P.S. Many thanks for the portrait of Mendelssohn. Remember
me to Magnus, and thank him for it.

Jenny refers above to a replica of a portrait of Mendelssohn
by Magnus, which the artist had presented to her. She subsequently bequeathed it to Mendelssohn's daughter, Mrs. Victor
Benecke.

After leaving Cuxhaven Jenny wrote once again :

IX

Nienstädten, September 3, 1846

Beloved Amalia :

I am wondering whether somehow or other I can manage to
visit you for a few days. For I long for you all with my whole
soul, and you would not believe, Amalia, what an impression
my stay in your house has left upon my inner life.

You will write to me soon, and tell me you are well. I shall
stay here a fortnight or three weeks longer. My good Louise
has been ill, and is not yet well enough for me to put a strain
upon her. So I am not going to begin my "guest-performances"
just yet.

The baths seem to have done me a great deal of good. I am
at Nienstädten again, and shall continue to rest here.

All good angels be with you! Farewell, dear friend. Do not
forget your for ever and ever loving and grateful

Jenny

Louise Johansson's illness proved to be a passing indisposition, and soon after the middle of September she accompanied
Jenny to Frankfurt, where engagements for the autumn season
had been arranged.

Once at Frankfurt, Jenny began keeping a systematic record

of all her performances. An "x" placed opposite a performance
indicated that the proceeds went in part or whole to charitable
causes. The number of such signs is a revelation of the singer's
unparallelled generosity. She kept a faithful record until her
marriage in February, 1852.

Holland and Rockstro print a letter written by Jenny to
Madame Birch-Pfeiffer on October 6, 1846, Jenny's twenty-
sixth birthday, but they omit entirely another letter sent to
Amalia on the same day :

X

October 6, 1846. Frankfurt

My beloved Amalia :

Imagine my joy when I came home today and found one
more place set at table. When I asked Louise who had come
she would not tell me, and finally our young man, my "brother"
Rudolph, came in!! Ah! It did my heart so much good. I
believe that everything that comes from you four—from you
five, I mean—finds its way directly to my heart.

I tell you, Amalia, it cuts me to the quick, for I can see so
clearly what he is going through. He has certainly grown very
thin. Now, therefore, your second son is very [illegible]. My
dear one! I share all your feelings. If you could only read my
innermost thoughts and see how every one of them is directed
to all of you. But, Amalia, it must certainly be the greatest
joy on this earth to be as dearly loved by one's children as you
are !

I would certainly have written to you long before, but I
thought that you and the family would be in Berlin towards the
eleventh or twelfth of October. Actually you wrote that you
would send me a letter then.

October 7 [same letter] :

Now he is sitting next to me, our "child", and is very much
at home and in reflective mood.[15] Dear soul! Give me the
pleasure of a couple of lines while I am in Darmstadt. I shall

[15] This is an approximate translation of a nearly illegible line.

stay there from the sixteenth to the eighteenth of this month at
the Traube.

You must tell me how you all are getting on. I am doing fine
and so is Louise. I love you as always, and this love rather in-
creases than diminishes.

Greetings once more to my Professor, and greetings to all
from

Your

Jenny

About this time Mendelssohn was trying to persuade Jenny
Lind to appear in London for a season at Her Majesty's
Theatre, which was under the direction of Mr. Benjamin Lumley. Jenny's English friends, among them Mrs. George Grote
and her brother, Edward Lewin, saw no insurmountable difficulties in the way of an engagement at Her Majesty's Theatre.
Jenny, however, was frightened even at the idea of setting foot
in London, for early in 1845 she had unwisely placed her signa-
ture to a document, at the urgent plea of Mr. Alfred Bunn of
the Drury Lane Theatre, to sing there, and she was now over-
due in meeting the requirements of this contract. At the time
of signing she was between acts in her role of Vielka[16] in Berlin—Bunn had sought her out in the box of the Earl of Westmorland. Because of the seeming haste of what he attempted to
make an emergency, and with the urging of the Ambassador,
Jenny Lind signed the "contract" handed to her, without benefit
of lawyer and without the careful appraisal of a discussion between friends. Probably Meyerbeer, too, urged her to go to
England to sing in *Das Feldlager in Schlesien,* for her interpretation in Berlin of the part (which he had written with Jenny
specifically in mind) was so brilliant, and had been received
with such rapture, that no doubt he was anxious to repeat the
triumph in London. Later on, the whole idea seemed so against
her interests that she could not force herself to fulfil the agreement. Meanwhile, Alfred Bunn had pressed the matter with
threatening letters.

It was at this point that her English friends and Mr. Lumley,

16 In Meyerbeer's *Das Feldlager in Schlesien.*

with the full sympathy of Mendelssohn, attempted to free Jenny from her paralyzing fear of appearing at all in England. Her terror was understandable, for there seems no doubt that, in her complete innocence of English law, she had been led to believe that if she did come to England she would be put in prison for breach of contract.

Mr. Lumley, a gentleman of trust, busied himself in every way, through personal journeys and through planning, to secure Jenny for Her Majesty's Theatre. He agreed to take on the responsibility for any legal damages arising from "l'affaire Bunn", assuming the risk personally for any sum levied against the singer. Moreover, he made the most detailed preparations possible for Jenny's comfort and welfare in London. Benjamin Lumley had a feeling of tremendous admiration and respect for the singer, apart from his natural wish that she should appear at his theatre.

After Frankfurt, her busy schedule took her to Darmstadt, where she sang three times at the Court Theatre between October 13 and 19. In accordance with the arrangement which she had outlined to Amalia Wichmann in the letter of August 1, she proceeded from Darmstadt to Munich, where, in late October and early November, she sang twice in *La Sonnambula,* once in *Norma,* once in *Der Freischütz* and twice in *La Figlia del Reggimento,* besides giving a concert for the benefit of the orchestra.

Towards the end of October, she sent the following letter from Munich to Rudolph Wichmann, who was preparing to enter Heidelberg University at this time—quite a remarkable letter from a young woman who had just turned twenty-six years of age. The date was either just before or just after a letter written on October 27 to Amalia Wichmann which we also quote below. There seems to be a possibility that the young man had developed an intense liking, a "heartache", for Jenny Lind which may account for the hint of family jealousy that seems to be expressed in the letter to Amalia. The letter to Rudolph is not among those in our collection.

XI

Munich, October, 1846

You are just going to begin life, dear Rudolph; and life has quite as much joy as it has sorrow : for my part I prefer the sorrow : for there is something exalted about it, whenever one's heart is full of pain : for then it is that we first feel how poor we are on earth, how rich in heaven.

This is the letter to Amalia Wichmann :

XII

Munich, October 27, 1846

A thousand thanks, my dear Amalia, for your kindness in executing my commission so soon and so quickly.[17] Once again my time was rather limited; otherwise I should have written to you immediately from Darmstadt. Everything went satisfactorily as planned. I hope that you are getting along splendidly and that I shall soon have news of those whom I love so much.

I was so frightened after your last letter that I did not dare to tell Rudolph when I passed through Heidelberg. It is hard for me, Amalia, to imagine that it could occur to anybody to be envious of my friendship; your peace of mind is after all too important to me and I like Rudolph too much ever to cause you any unpleasantness. Oh! it hurt me to pass through Heidelberg by train in the evening and not see Rudolph.

But everything has something of good in it, and I was glad not to have to say farewell to him a second time. It is really heavenly there in its beautiful natural setting.

Now let me tell you that I am going to London, and that Mendelssohn alone was able to persuade me to do so. For you know what confidence I place in his advice; and, besides, things have really so shaped themselves that I can clearly see that God Himself has so ordained it—and against one's destiny one can do nothing.

[17] The commission was for rouge. In Berlin, critics had suggested that she should use it more freely on the stage, which she was always reluctant to do.

I shall not sing much longer in Germany. I remain in Vienna until about the middle of February; and then I go to Italy for five or six weeks.[18] Tell me, therefore, where Herrmann [now Professor and Musik-director by title] is living; so that if possible we may meet. I go to Florence, Siena and Rome. Perhaps he may be in the neighbourhood. How I rejoice that the time is approaching! These journeys round and round! Oh, dear, good Amalia!

I saw Schubner-Wagen. She was so very nice to me, and meeting her did me much good.

I am living with the Kaulbachs[19] and am very happy here. He is a dear, dear man, and his wife is very lovable. I have lighted upon the best house in Munich, as I did in Berlin.

Besides this, it goes well with me here, as it does everywhere. I am beginning to get used to this, though I cannot conceive what it is that satisfies people. But that is God's doing.

Greetings to my Professor and youngest "child" and dear "brother". And I hold you to your word to return me your love.

Ever yours
Jenny

(P.S.) Many greetings to Professor Werder. I will write to Taubert as soon as possible. My address is c/o Prof. Kaulbach, Obergartenstrasse 16½.

At the home of Professor Kaulbach Jenny was brought into contact with the leading men and women of Bavaria. At that time Kaulbach was engaged in the preparation of his splendid edition of Goethe's *Reinecke Fuchs*.

Among those who came to the Kaulbach home were Herr Franz Hauser, Director of the Munich Conservatoire; Professor Lassaulx, who held the Chair of Philology at the University of Munich; Herr Joseph von Görres, Professor of History in the same University; Dr. Georg Phillips, Professor of Jurisprudence

---

[18] In her contract with Mr. Lumley he undertook to pay her £800 in case she wanted to spend some time in Italy studying the language before her London season. In the event, however, she did not feel this to be necessary.

[19] Professor Wilhelm von Kaulbach was a well-known Bavarian painter.

at the University; and Herr Gasser, a young sculptor with a bright future.

Jenny had engagements to fulfil in Stuttgart between November 11 and 22, and after that she went to Karlsruhe, where she sang on three occasions. While there, she sent the following letter to Amalia:

XIII

Karlsruhe, Nov. 28, 1846

My Much-Loved Amalia!

You know how my time is occupied; and I do not need to tell you that this is the cause of my long silence.

But you have given me much to think about, and I have been racking my brains to find a reason that would seem plausible to everybody as to why I must be with you in Berlin in the month of September or October. Thank you for wanting me to come, and I promise you that I will not leave Germany without seeing you once again.

Whatever may happen at your home to all of you, may heaven ordain and direct everything for the good of all. To be allowed to be your child, your sister, your friend, dear Amalia, means more to me than you can ever imagine. For my heart will steadfastly abide with you throughout eternity! Yes, indeed. If only I were back with you again! How often I think of you, and how happy I am when I think of that beautiful time when I was with all of you. Remembrance is vivid; but it can only feel longing for the reality.

I am once more in the neighbourhood of Heidelberg, and I have been asked to give a concert there, but I don't know how I shall fit it in.

Our Rudolph wrote to me recently, and I will soon write to him, too. God protect you all in this unkind world. Otto [Wichmann] is the luckiest of us all! But the time will come probably for him too, poor boy.

Tell me, Amalia, has Herrmann really fallen so deeply in love with a Roman girl? Heavens! What do you mean? What misfortune will this bring to your family? I am not being inquisitive. You need not give me an answer to this question before you want to.

I am astonished at what you told me concerning *Taubert*. Just why did he go to Vienna, when he knew quite well how things would be with her? I was frightfully sorry about it. How human beings fail to cherish their happiness!

Rellstab has written me a splendid letter, which has given me great pleasure—though I still hold firm, tell him—and matters remain as they were.[20] Remember me most kindly to him and his wife when next you see them.

Yes! . . . If only it were all over in London! But the thought that it will be the LAST will strengthen me.

God be with you all. A thousand greetings to my Professor. He must just write me a few words at Christmas. Oh! beg him! —beg him!

For ever yours,
Jenny

(P.S.) Oh! Tell Dr Mendelssohn that he must not quite forget me, I beg. And great Mlle. Billarde.

In a fortnight I shall be in Munich again; and after that in Vienna, about the 22-24 December.

Louise sends all possible greetings. Many greetings to the Schrödens, [one name here is illegible], Früderüch, and also to Count Roedern, who plays[21] the piano so beautifully. Did he not play too?

Give Otto, too, my friendly greetings.

After leaving Karlsruhe Jenny proceeded to Heidelberg, where, on December 5, she sang in a concert with such success that a gathering of students serenaded her at her lodgings and paraded with torches. The next day found her on her way to Mannheim, and that evening she appeared there in *La Figlia del Reggimento*. Proceeding to Nuremberg, she sang on December 9 in *La Sonnambula*, and two days later once more in

---

[20] Ludwig Rellstab, poet and famous critic, and author of the libretto of *Das Feldlager in Schlesien*. Here he was attempting to persuade Jenny Lind not to carry out her wish to leave the stage.

[21] The word is scrawled and completely illegible, but we are using the verb that conveys the obvious meaning.

La Figlia del Reggimento. Her visit to the last place was commemorated by the striking of a gold medal in her honour.

Soon she was in Augsburg, singing in the last concert at which she was to appear before her return to Munich. The long trip was made in deep snow, but the "Child of the North" was quite used to ice, snow and grey skies.

The first railway ever constructed in Germany—from Nuremberg to Fürth—had been operating for ten years, and it was on this line that Jenny Lind was able to travel when she left Augsburg.

In Munich she was engaged to sing in operas that included *Don Giovanni* and *Le Nozze di Figaro.* Christmas, once again, was spent away from home, but the whole world by this time was her friend. She sang in Haydn's *Creation,* which was given on Christmas Day.

Her travels brought her to Vienna, where she arrived on the last day of the year. She was saddened to learn that Mme. Vivanot, in whose home she had previously been so happily welcomed, was dead. Therefore, she chose to stay in some apartments attached to the *Theater an der Wien* which she rented from Herr Pokorny.

Among her friends in Vienna were the Countess Schönborn and her sister the Countess Ruenburg, besides the poet-dramatist Grillparzer. Perhaps her closest friends were the family of Herr Oberstabsarzt Professor Dr. von Jaeger, a respected physician, whose daughter was Jenny's intimate associate and whose wife was like a mother to both young women. Whatever time she had free in the Vienna season of 1847 she spent with these friends, in later life always recalling these days as some of her happiest.

Robert and Clara Schumann were also in Vienna, giving concerts. Jenny Lind, now their devoted friend, lost no time in offering to sing at one of these. She made herself a loving friend of the young Schumann children, who would sit in her lap when she came to call. One afternoon, when the Schumanns were visiting Jenny, she made Clara promise that they would never go to Stockholm unless she were there to greet them and sing with them.

While she was in Vienna she wrote to Amalia :

XIV

January 7, 1847, Vienna

If I only knew how to thank you, my beloved Amalia! How did I ever deserve all this from you?

I simply cannot tell you how happy your gifts made us. Just think, on New Year's Eve we arrived here and immediately received the things you had sent. I was so happy that I just can't express my feelings—that you had thought of *us*, and in such a way! This lace, dear Amalia, what can I say about it? Indeed, I accept it all with love and thankfulness, and this is the only reward I can give you.

Give dear Otto my best thanks. I will write to him very soon. I can't do so today, for I am appearing here for the first time again.

At first I didn't like your picture very much—but the more I look at it the more it seems to resemble you, and now I am delighted with it. How nice it is always to have before your eyes somebody whom you love. Thank you, dear Otto. I also owe many thanks to my Professor for the little letter, which made me so happy.

How everything in this world changes! And poor Vivanot, in whose house I lived the last time, has recently died. Now I am living with the Pokornys.

Oh! Amalia—this year I shall see you all again and escape from the stage. My prayer is that our reunion will find us well and gay. May you and your family always be happy. Dear Amalia, my heart beats for you and yours. May your love for me be steadfast. I cannot cherish a better wish in my breast!

Farewell! Greet all my friends and especially Herr von Berg,[22] and keep enfolded in your rich love your deeply loving

Jenny

P.S. It's up to you to decide about the copy of the picture. If you have no objections, I like it as it is. Arrange this with Herr Magnus and give him my most cordial greetings. *Do exactly as you like about it.*[23]

[22] Jenny's first singing master.

[23] This postscript must refer to the famous portrait of her by Professor Magnus, which she had commissioned him to execute as a special gift to

(Note written along the side of the first page :) Louise thanks you and sends many greetings!

Meyerbeer had been working for some time on a revised version of *Das Feldlager in Schlesien* which was put into active rehearsal at the *Theater an der Wien* and first performed on February 18, 1847. There had been certain changes in the libretto in order to make it more acceptable to a Viennese audience. The new title, *Vielka,* seemed to carry a certain appeal.

Its success carried it through an immediate run of thirteen nights. The *Wiener Zeitung* for February 26, 1847, had this to say about it (we quote an English translation made before the turn of the century) :

"Jenny Lind appears, in the role of Vielka, excellently great both as a singer and an actress. As loveliest among the lovely touches in her exalted theme, and finest among the fine, we may call special attention, in the First Act, to the song with the Rondo, sung with elfish spirit and charming gracefulness; in the Third Act, to the solo, with the flute-duet, in which Vielka sings now before, and now after, the flutes. Jenny Lind sang this piece in such sort, that out of the flute-duet a flute-trio was elaborated; developing her masterly passages like an uninterrupted row of pearls, in an unsurpassable manner, so tender, so melting, so certain that the public was truly enchanted and bewitched."

Among the honours extended to Jenny Lind in Vienna, between January and April, 1847, was a soirée given on March 7 by the Russian Grand Duchess. On March 17 the Archduchess Sophia gave a concert at which Jenny sang Haydn's

---

the Wichmann family, in grateful recognition of the many pleasant hours spent under their roof. Fifteen years later, at the request of Otto Goldschmidt, Magnus copied his original painting with such dexterity that the copy could not be distinguished from the original. Eventually the latter found its place in the Berlin National Gallery.

Many imitations and copies were made of it; among them were prints, oil paintings, drawings, etc., fashioned in a manner similar to the Magnus portrait. It became the best-known pose of the singer, almost a trade-mark. A French Haviland china bust, closely following the lines of the portrait, is a typical example of the popularity of Magnus' image of Jenny Lind.

"Nun beut die Flur", Mozart's "Sull' Aria" (with Mlle. Wil-
dauer), Bellini's "Casta Diva", and the unaccompanied trio from
Roberto il Diavolo, "Unsel'ger Augenblick" (with Herren von
Marchion and Staudigl).

As usual, performances were given for the benefit of in-
dividual friends and for charity in general.

The following letter illustrates Jenny's lifetime loyalty to
Amalia:

XV

Vienna, January 20, 1847

Dearest Amalia:

I know your love and self-denying kindness for me so well
that I do not for a moment fear you will be vexed if I send
someone to your house. Is it not so? You will not be angry with
me?

I mean the Schumanns.

You know, of course, that her talent is altogether splendid;
for of course you have often heard of her as Clara Wieck. They
are two such excellent and noble, really noble persons that they
will give you great pleasure. Please, dearest, receive these two
dear people kindly, and as friends, for your own sake, and for
mine. The wife is very sensitive, and you will see that she is a
quite exceptional woman. He is a composer *plein d'esprit,* and
modest to the last degree. I asked them if they had any acquaintances in Berlin; and they seemed to me to have no real ones.
So then I thought of you; and you will know how grateful I
shall be.

Ah, yes! When shall I see you again? *Mon Dieu!* This longing for rest grows upon me almost unbearably; but time passes
quickly, and no mortal will be so glad as I, when I am free.

Jenny

Three weeks later another letter was sent to Amalia:

XVI

Vienna, February 13, 1847

Dearly Beloved :

What can you be thinking about! I, going to Paris! Never as long as I live. Who could have told you that? And how could I have entertained such an idea, without telling you![24]

No, dearest Amalia. Not only am I not going to Paris, but it seems as if I shall not even go to London.

Bunn will not give up the contract; and I cannot go there unless he does so, for he actually threatens to put me in prison ! ! ! I tell you, Amalia, I should be *wild* with joy, if I had not to go there ! *Mon Dieu!* Just suppose this happened !

They have made me all kinds of offers from Paris; but I did not have to give it a moment's thought.

I will leave the stage—and then I shall want nothing else in the world.

How are all you beloved people? Good heavens! How long it has been since I saw you. But I love you, Amalia, and so much that I wish you would put me to the test some time. My good, true, faithful Louise is well again. She has suffered so much from toothache.

I am quite well; and it goes more than well with me here. *Das Feldlager* is not yet ready, but it is to be given next week, and everything is going very well. The Opera will certainly create a *furore* here in Vienna.

Today is one of those days, my beloved Amalia, when I feel so lonely in this world without a protector to whom I can turn and see my own love returned in his loving glances. Oh, the pure love between husband and wife is after all—it must be— the most sublime of feelings, and a real necessity for us human beings. I have a loving soul. I should like very much to make someone happy, for I feel within myself the power to do so. But where does one find the right man?

I rejoice that it gives me so much pleasure to hear of Viardot

---

[24] No doubt Jenny is so emphatic because, during the ten months which she spent in Paris under the tuition of Garcia, she had been lonely and unhappy, and had found extremely uncongenial the gay life of the fashionable world.

Garcia's[25] success in Berlin. I have never been envious for a
moment. Tell Taubert so : he thinks me rather weak on that
point.

>   For ever and ever, with my whole heart,
>   Your loving
>   Jenny

A few weeks later she wrote again :

XVII

>   Vienna, March 26, 1847

I have got to go to London. Will you send me a few words
to Munich by the next mail? I shall be there soon, staying with
the Kaulbachs.

How wonderfully everything has gone for me, here in Vienna!
And how nice it would be for me if I had not to go to London.
But even that may have its good side!

Thanks, a thousand thanks for your last letter. It made me so
happy to hear that their Majesties the King and Queen [of
Prussia] wish to hear me again that I was moved to tears. You
must know, dear Amalia, that my heart is so bound to these
Royal persons, so filled with thanks for the sympathy that I
found at the Prussian Court, when I came there a stranger and
unknown, that, for the Queen especially, I would pass through
fire, if she desired me. To me, therefore, every wish of the King
or Queen is sacred, and I beg you to tell Graf von Redern that
I will gratefully fulfil this as soon as possible. Ah! to see you
and them again, Amalia! and to talk with you in peace! My
heart bounds at the thought!

Jenny's arrival in London and her great success there are now
a part of operatic history—though, even after she had conquered
her fear of coming to England, she could not at first bring herself to sing. For some time she kept Mr. Lumley, her friends and

---

[25] Viardot Garcia was a daughter of Jenny Lind's singing master in
Paris. Both Viardot and her better-known sister, Marietta Garcia Malibran,
enjoyed considerable repute as singers.

musical London on tenterhooks, while she spent the days in des-
perate indecision; and it was only when she understood that
the theatre was losing money daily—since everyone hung back
and refused to buy tickets until her appearance was announced
—that she conquered her hesitation and set the day when she
would sing. Once she had made up her mind and begun rehears-
ing, her uncertainties and distress vanished. Her initial appearance at Her Majesty's Theatre on May 4, 1847, in *Roberto il
Diavolo* created an excitement never before witnessed by the
oldest frequenter of the theatre. When the doors were opened
at half-past seven there was a terrific crush. Ladies were carried
off their feet, and they and their escorts were shoved against
columns and walls. The standing room section was in chaos,
with persons unable even to get a glimpse of the singer. The
Queen, the Prince Consort, the Queen Dowager and the Duchess
of Kent occupied the Royal boxes to the left of the stage. Mendelssohn and his friend, Mrs. Grote's husband, sat in the stalls.
Fanny Kemble and other persons of note were given special
places. The triumph was complete when Her Majesty sent a
superb arrangement of flowers to the stage as Jenny made her
bows.

This triumph and many others were achieved not only by
her unassailable technique and the marvellous quality of her
voice, but also by her ability to identify herself completely with
the character which she was portraying on the stage. A conversation recorded with an established critic concerning her
superb rendering of Alice in *Roberto il Diavolo* illustrates this
uncanny empathy. When asked by this critic how she had
achieved such a magnificent characterization in the role of Alice,
Jenny Lind replied: "How could I tell how I sang it? I stood
at the man's right hand, and the Fiend at his left, and all I could
think of was how to save him."

During the opera season Jenny Lind consented to tour the
provinces, and on such trips the brother of her dear Mrs. Grote,
Edwin Lewin, took charge of affairs, for he was familiar with
Swedish and French. It is impossible in this little book, devoted
to Jenny's letters to Amalia Wichmann, to attempt to do jus-
tice to the remarkable acclaim given her in England during the
year 1847, and this portion of her career we must leave to the

biographers. We need say only that such a reception in England was unparallelled in the annals of the opera.

In the summer of 1847 Jenny wrote to Amalia as follows:

XVIII

London, Clairville, Old Brompton, July 25, 1847

My Beloved Amalia:

I hope that you never doubt my boundless love for you, although I am a very bad correspondent. It would be hard if you were not convinced that I shall love you always and for all time. A thousand thanks for your last letter. May you all be well and in good spirits.

That was certainly terribly about Hensel.[26] It gave me quite a shock. It is good that Mendelssohn has finally gone to Switzerland with his family.

A few days ago I received a very nice letter from Kustner. You know how friendly he always was to me. I am quite sure that he is a good and honest man; and I shall write—which is a great deal from me!—to tell him that I cannot stay long in Berlin, or sing more than two or three times at the utmost, as I leave England so late—not until nearly the end of September. We cannot, therefore, be long together, dearly beloved, as I must get to Sweden before the weather becomes too bad.

Do you know, the Professor's likeness of me[27] has pleased the Queen immensely—and now I must ask a very great favour. Lablache is also so enchanted with the portrait that I have been obliged to promise him that I will ask the Professor to let him

[26] Jenny writes "Helselt", perhaps an absent-minded substitution for the person obviously intended, Fanny Hensel, the beloved sister of Felix Mendelssohn, who had died very suddenly on May 14th. Her death was a severe blow to him. He was already debilitated by overwork and illness, and this great loss must certainly have been a contributory cause to his own death about six months later (November 4th).

[27] The marble medallion-portrait by Professor Wichmann, impressed upon the binding of each of the two volumes of Holland and Rockstro. This had been executed during the previous summer, when Jenny sprained her ankle while she was staying with the Wichmanns, and was forced to rest for three weeks.

have a copy of it. I shall be eternally obliged if my Professor will let me have a little head—you know what I mean : *my* head—for Lablache. He will be here till the middle of August. Ah! I entreat you, do me this great kindness. He has begged so hard for it.

Do not be angry with me for writing so fervently and so badly. I am, believe me, for all time

For ever yours,
Jenny

P.S. We are quite well. I am enchanted with England.

Along the side of this letter Jenny has written : "Special greetings to my Professor, Otto, and to the Heidelberger [Rudolph Wichmann]."

And again : "It would be best to send the picture direct to me, Clairville, Old Brompton, London."

The Lablache referred to in this letter is Signor Luigi Lablache (1794-1858), father of the Frédéric Lablache who sang with Jenny Lind on her tour of America and on many later occasions in Europe. The elder Lablache, himself a famous bass who had sung in all the major opera houses of Europe and had been Queen Victoria's singing teacher, proved to be a devoted admirer and helpful friend of Jenny Lind from their first meeting at Lumley's theatre shortly after her arrival in England.

As she states in this letter, Jenny Lind could not leave England until the autumn because of the extended tour she was about to make—one that would take her all the way from Brighton to Edinburgh and back. Among the most interesting of her visits were the few days which she spent at Norwich, where she gave at least three concerts. The Bishop of Norwich, the Right Reverend Edward Stanley, an ardent music lover and long an admirer of Jenny Lind from afar, invited her to stay at his home, the Bishop's palace, during her visit to Norwich. What had happened in Berlin on a deeper scale with the Wichmanns recurred here in miniature. The Bishop, his wife, his son, his guests, and even the servants all lost their hearts to Jenny Lind. Each one found a special quality to admire in her, and the ever adaptable Jenny, intuitively sensing these personal approaches to her art, always found the right words and tone with which to respond to them.

An excellent example of her humorous resiliency in almost any situation was her response to the Bishop's son, Arthur Stanley, afterwards Dean of Westminster, who gives the following account of this episode. We quote from his letter describing it to a friend.

"On the last day, I told her that there was 'quelque chose d'extraordinaire dans la voix', but that, otherwise, her singing, in itself, produced no impression whatever upon me. This, she said, was by far the most amusing thing she had heard, and that she should never forget it."

It would be even more amusing to know what Jenny was really thinking at that moment. But what finesse she used to transform this musical Philistine's parting remark into a charming farewell!

But before she set out on her tour of the provinces she wrote to Amalia again:

XIX

August 12, 1847. Clairville, Old Brompton
Dearest and Beloved Amalia:

You believe, I see, that I am engaged to someone! How should this be? And to whom? I am sure I know nobody whom I would have! And I have very high thoughts of finding a being to whom I could utterly and entirely surrender myself in love. No!—it is not true that I am going to marry, dear, dearest Amalia! I cannot give you this joy. Ah! if I could find a man such as you are a woman—then, indeed, I should be lost!

How delighted I am that I have finished here! For it is better to look back upon the accomplishment of so great a thing than to look forward to it. The English public has been unexampled in its kindness to me.

This was followed on September 30, 1847, by a brief note:

XX

I leave my beloved England next Thursday, the 5th. I cannot, however, tell the exact day of my arrival in Berlin. I will write again from Hamburg.

On the evening of Jenny's departure from England she had supper with a group consisting of Mr. Lumley and Mr. and Mrs. Grote, after which the party went by carriage to the Custom House Stairs. There they took a small wherry and conducted the singer on board the Hamburg Packet, *John Bull*. The three who took leave of her did so with the happy thought that Jenny Lind had consented to return to England, for Mr. Lumley had induced her to contract for a second engagement at Her Majesty's Theatre.

During the visit to Berlin which followed, her third, Jenny Lind sang only four times on the stage, once at a Court Concert, and again at a concert for the Chorus of the Opera. Taubert had composed the song for the last occasion, *Ich muss nun enmal singen*. Rellstab wound up his long and elaborate critique of this concert as follows : [28]

"Deep emotion was to be read in the demeanour of the beloved artist, who had won the hearts, as well as the highest admiration, of all.

"If what life bestows upon her equals what she has adorned it with in such rich abundance, then her days will be overarched by Heaven with purer happiness than it is given to many to enjoy. For all that Art has become to us through her, in beauty, in elevation, in inspiration, our thanks be expressed in this wish for her future life. We know well that thousands will share it."

King Frederick William IV of Prussia, following the court concert given on October 16, appointed Mlle. Lind to the rank of *Kammersängerin* (court singer), taking the trouble to pen a little note to the singer himself, apart from the formal announcement made through Graf von Redern.

Jenny Lind left Berlin on October 19, pausing to sing *La Figlia del Reggimento* once at the Stadt-Theater in Hamburg on the twentieth, after which she proceeded to her beloved Stockholm. Her letter to Amalia follows :

[28] From the *Königliche priv. Berliner (Vossische) Zeitung*, i.e., the *Royal Gazette of Berlin*, October 20, 1847.

XXI

Stockholm, December 15, 1847

Beloved Amalia :

A word from your Jenny. She hasn't yet become reasonable. She is only mourning the friend whom she will never see again, and she scarcely knows how to find consolation.[29] Oh! what a blow, Amalia! And what a fate hangs over us human beings! You see—he was the only person to whom I felt myself so completely devoted! The only person who brought fulfilment to my spirit, and almost as soon as I found him I lost him again.

But I want to talk of something else now. Christmas is just round the corner, and how well I remember Christmas night two years ago! May you all remain healthy and happy together, and may the dear Lord send you all good things.

Think of me when you can. I am in such a strange mood today. I am so happy and so quiet, at home again. It suits me so well; and the people are my own country-folk; and they love me for that.

I have no fear of feeling any void, for I can do much good here, and have already begun to set about it.

My aunt is very nice. Do let me hear from all of you soon, and never doubt that I remain for my whole life your most sincerely loving

Jenny

P.S. Greet my dear brother and my father. When are the boys going to write to me? My dear, kindly forward this letter. I don't know their address.

In a few days' time another letter was sent, immediately after Christmas but with no exact day given :

XXII

Stockholm, December 1847

Dear Amalia :

You are an angel to me! How can I thank you enough for having thought of me at Christmas time. I am quite delighted with the picture. It is an unbelievable likeness. Oh! I am so

---

[29] The reference is to Mendelssohn's death six weeks earlier.

very fond of both of them. I do hope that they are all well. What
is Herrmann doing? Give him my warmest greetings. How happy
I am that His Majesty the King has spoken about me. Berlin is
and still remains very dear to my heart.

I see everyone so clearly—the house—really everything, and
my soul is delighted by this memory. In addition, I am getting
along very well. Even though I am having a bit of trouble with
my heart. This is not so easy, but the Good Lord usually helps
when one needs help most. I will, of course, tell you all about
this some time.

When shall we see each other again? No more trips to
Hanover! If we are now friends, Amalia, what does it matter
to us that the world wishes it otherwise? All the worse for
these poor envious creatures.

Give my warm greetings to Viardot. Tell her that I have
never doubted that she is a splendid and magnificent woman,
and that it never occurred to me to compare her with the vast
majority of ordinary artists, that is, with most of the women
singers of today. I am delighted that we shall see each other
in London.

Taubert is really heavenly. I can see his face now as he left
with the picture. Only don't say that I said so.

I remain for you and for all of you the same loving,

Jenny

This little letter is to two of the Wichmann sons:

XXIII

February 1848. Stockholm

Do you know, dear brothers, it has been beautiful in Stockholm this winter; heaps of snow, and that is just what makes our
city beautiful. I am gay: and then again, not so gay. I do not
quite know what I ought to do—whether to set off on my
travels again, or stay here always. I am hoping that perhaps we
may take a journey together.

Jenny's main purpose during her visit to her native Sweden

was to earn money for the establishing of scholarships or stipends for worthy young students in the fields of music, painting, sculpture and architecture. From the time that she won her place in the larger European musical world—that is, since her first successes in Berlin in 1845—she never appropriated for her own use any of the money that she subsequently earned in her native land, but donated every penny of her earnings there to worthy musical causes. She always felt a deep sense of gratitude to the State of Sweden for the generous manner in which it had taken her—a poor, young, fledgling singer—under its protecting wing; and throughout her life she continued to repay this self-imposed debt of honour. Thus, between December, 1847, and April, 1848, she raised for this purpose the sum of twenty-two thousand Swedish dollars, which was placed in the hands of two trustees, one of them being her faithful guardian and close friend Judge Munthe. At the time of her death the amount had increased considerably, and it was divided between the Royal Academy of Music and the Royal Academy of Fine Arts. By the years 1885 to 1890 many promising young students had been given the assistance needed to establish themselves.

The only event that marred her happiness in Sweden was the news about the suit brought against her by Mr. Bunn in London. On February 23, 1848, the case was heard in London before Sir W. Erle, sitting in the Court of Queen's Bench. It ended in the award of £2,500 to Mr. Bunn, which Mr. Lumley had agreed to pay. The whole affair was, of course, quite distasteful to Jenny Lind, whose innocence of business matters was the main cause of her entanglement with the law.

Jenny's father and mother, who were almost estranged but who had been enabled to live more comfortably by their daughter's regular financial aid and her gift of a home in the country, arrived in Stockholm to hear Jenny sing in l'Elisir d'Amore. They could not move in their daughter's world, for they would have found themselves ill at ease in any gathering such as that which she enjoyed so much at the Wichmanns' in Berlin. During her stay in Stockholm Jenny Lind was made welcome everywhere in circles where birth and position are considered of importance, as well as in others where character and intelligence are basic elements for acceptance. Jenny her-

self was a part of such company not because of her background
and education but rather because of her genius, beauty of personality, and ability to acquire the culture denied her in early
home life. By the time she had reached her thirties she could
write letters in four languages, and express herself quite well in
any one of them.

Mendelssohn's recent death still lay heavily on her mind at
this time. She could not persuade herself to sing a *Lied* of this
great musician for two years afterwards.

There was, though, a happy note which may have counter-
balanced her sadness. She was delighted at the thought of soon
returning to London, and her plans included taking with her her
old music master, Herr Berg, his wife and their young daughter.

In March, 1848, a note of worry crept into her writing, for
we find this brief letter among those in our collection:

XXIV

March 28, 1848. Stockholm

For Heaven's sake, Amalia, let me know immediately how
you are all faring. I am desperately anxious about you.

I leave Stockholm on the 13th of April. Before that time,
please think of your loving

Jenny

Her anxiety, of course, was caused by the March revolution
of 1848.

Early on an afternoon in April Jenny Lind left Sweden on
the steamer "Gauthiod", which sailed from Skeppsbron amidst
the cheering and waving of the crowd. The opera choir took
their place in barges near the steamer, so that they might
serenade the departing artist. In another boat, the Uplands
regimental band performed airs from the operas in which Jenny
Lind had sung in Sweden. With her, in place of Louise, whom
she had pensioned off, was Josephina Ahmansson, a cousin of
Fru Berg. Upon her arrival on April 21 in London, where she
stayed once again at Clairville Cottage, she was greeted with
all the enthusiasm that had prevailed in 1847. Mr. Lumley

noted in his diary that all London knew of Jenny's arrival, and that the same fever-heat was generated as at her former appearance.

In Lumley's *Reminiscences of the Opera* (pp. 218-19) he speaks of the excitement created by the singer at Her Majesty's Theatre. There were struggling crowds early at the doors; hats were ruined, dresses torn; carriages, policemen, coachmen and servants were thrown into confusion outside.

On May 25 Jenny Lind appeared in *Lucia di Lammermoor*. The long and enthusiastic account in *The Times* on May 26 sums up the feelings of all those lucky enough to hear her:

"Last night was the most remarkable one of the season. Mlle. Lind appeared, for the first time, in *Lucia di Lammermoor*, and raised to the highest enthusiasm the immense audience that had attended. . . .

"The audience were kept in a state of the greatest excitement; and plaudits, repeated calls, and bouquets marked their unbounded delight."

Three weeks later she wrote to Amalia:

XXV

London, June 21, 1848

Dearest Amalia:

I am depending on your kindness, and especially upon your friendship, not to think that I have forgotten you, or anything like that, but you should put my silence down to laziness.

I have received your letter and thank you for it with all my heart.

Recent political events have been so turbulent that I have been forced to do some very serious thinking about the state of our world. I believe, my dear "Mathilda", that many changes are going to take place, and that we shall see a number of new political developments before 1848 is over. May God grant that we shall soon have peace again in the world, for the present uncertainty is quite terrible for everybody.

How often and how earnestly I think of you all and of my boys! How much it pains me to learn that they are actually

soldiers now—a trend of these parlous times! Do they talk about
me still? What is Rudolph doing? What is my professor doing?
And both the others? And my Vienna! Oh, God, how sorry I
am for what is happening there!

But I don't want just to write painful things. I want to say
that I hope we shall all see each other again happy and healthy.
I hope you are as well as I am. Things still go splendidly with
me.

Well, our friend Pauline Viardot did not do too well with the
opera.

I have a charming Swedish family with me here, namely, my
first singing-master and his wife and daughter; so I am quite
comfortable, and in very cheerful company. They laugh and
talk all round, even at this very moment; so that I hardly know
what I am writing about.

Paul Taglioni was good enough to ask me whether I had
any errands in Berlin for him to execute, and therefore I must
hurry. I will say goodbye for today, and assure you with the
most sincere truth, that I could never forget how dear your
friendship is to me, and that I am devoted to you all with my
whole heart.

Your true,
Jenny

The Paul Taglioni mentioned in the letter above was an artist
of real ability, the brother of a famous *danseuse,* a descendant
on his mother's side of the Swedish tragedian Karsten, and well
known in Paris and in Berlin as a skilful composer of ballets.
Years later, Jenny Lind told her son that it was Taglioni who
had influenced Meyerbeer to persuade her to sing in Berlin.

Jenny Lind did not perform in *I Puritani* until the year 1848.
She had seen it at Her Majesty's Theatre in 1847, sitting next
to her friend Mrs. Grote, to whom she had whispered: "I think
I can do as well as that, and perhaps a little better." Anyone
attempting this opera was under a severe handicap, for in 1835,
at Her Majesty's Theatre, a wealth of talent had assembled to
put it over: Madame Grisi, Rubini, Tamburini and Lablache,
each one given a part exactly suited to his or her own powers.

The result was so spectacular that for many years this opera season was spoken of as the "Puritani season".

Yet here was Jenny Lind, supported only by the splendid Lablache, attempting to put over something which had previously required special voices in every part. *The Times* for July 31, 1848, proclaims her success :

"Her Elvira in *I Puritani,* which was performed on Saturday, was another triumph. It was not like any other Elvira which had been seen on the stage. The artlessness of the loving young girl, waiting, with sparkling eyes, for the arrival of her lover, was exquisitely rendered; and when the innocent hilarity of Elvira was interrupted in its course, by the sudden attack of insanity, the change was admirably elaborated. . . .

"The vocal triumph was as great as the histrionic. The sparkling polacca, executed to perfection, and with a playfulness which was completely illustrative of the character, electrified the audience, and was encored with an enthusiasm which is rarely heard in any theatre. In the mad scenes, an expression of wildness was apparent, even in the crying, and added to the stronger mournfulness of the situation. At the conclusion of the opera she was called repeatedly, and bouquets were thrown in showers."

Although the season was far advanced, *I Puritani* was given five times. The Queen and Prince Albert, always ardent admirers of Jenny Lind, continued their attendance to the end of the season.

Mr. Lumley was greatly pleased at the results of the season of 1848, which proved financially rewarding to him as well as a personally happy event. He noted in his record, "The curtain fell at last; and in falling, closed a season of unexampled interest."

Typical of Jenny Lind's charity was the concert for the benefit of the Brompton Hospital for Consumption and Diseases of the Chest, given on July 31, 1848. The hospital was a stone's throw from Clairville Cottage, where constant visitors included Mrs. Grote, Mr. and Mrs. Samuel Carter Hall, living close by, who were active in many charitable causes, Thalberg, the talented musician, and of course the Bergs, who had accompanied Jenny from Sweden. All of them joined in enthusiam for the hospital benefit, which would result, it was hoped, in a new wing to contain many more beds for patients. Mr. Lumley gave his special permission to Jenny Lind, releasing her from a restraining clause in the contract, and agreed to turn over Her Majesty's Theatre for the event. It is interesting to note that Otto Goldschmidt, Jenny's future husband, took part in the concert.

Upon the successful conclusion of this programme, the singer was presented with a magnificent silver salver, twenty inches across, bearing many words of appreciation. (It was inherited years afterwards by Madame Goldschmidt's second son.)

Earlier in the month Jenny Lind had attended one of Chopin's *matinées* in London and was most enthusiastic about him, both as a composer and as a performer. This admiration was mutual, for some two months earlier Chopin had met Jenny Lind and she had presented him with a stall for *La Sonnambula*. He found her voice infallibly pure and true, and thought that she possessed all "the magic rays of an *aurora borealis*".

Her Majesty's Theatre closed the season of 1848 on August 26, but once again there were plans for Jenny to tour the English provinces. She wrote to Amalia:

XXVI

Clairville, September 4, 1848

Beloved Amalia:

I was not a little astonished when I received your last letter from Interlaken. I was as happy as a queen to know that you are leaving Berlin *at this time,* even though your two sons do not feel at all as I do about it. My heart bounds with joy when I think of meeting you in Italy or elsewhere. Perhaps this time our long-cherished idea may be realized after all.

I am afraid that you did not receive the letter which Taglioni took with him when he left here. I am sorry about that. But to come quickly to the point now.

My head is full of plans, and, in case rest should again be denied me, I may still have to go on working.

Today I begin by going to the provinces here, for two, or

perhaps three, months. After that something is starting which
I want to tell you about.

I wish, in conjunction with one of Mendelssohn's most
intimate friends, to contribute towards a Music School in Germany in his memory; and for this purpose I propose to give a
grand concert in London in November.

If it is quiet in Berlin now, I might give concerts there also,
and so on and on and on—for how long I cannot say. But in
any case I hope to be finished with it all by the new year at
the latest.

Now be sweet, sota älskade, and write to me soon, to tell me
what you are doing and where you are going. Send your letter
here to London—Clairville Cottage, Old Brompton—and then
I shall be able to tell your something for certain.

God guard you!

Yours,

Jenny

There seems little doubt that the person to whom Jenny refers
as "one of Mendelssohn's most intimate friends" was none other
than Carl Klingemann. In the beautiful two-volume work, *The
Mendelssohn Family, 1729-1847* by Sebastian Hensel, Felix
Mendelssohn's nephew, the English translation of which was published by Harper and Brothers, New York, in 1882, we find this
reference to Klingemann : "He was one of the most prominent
and most faithful of the circle [that is, the Mendelssohn family
and their intimate friends]. The ties of friendship which united
him to the family were strengthened by Felix's and Hensel's
frequent visits to London, where Klingemann was attached to
the Hanoverian legation, and by a constant animated correspondence."

Some of the other interested friends were Herr Ferdinand
David, the violinist and frequent companion of Felix Mendelssohn, Mr. (later Sir) Julius Benedict, Mr. Buxton of the publishing firm of Ewer & Company, and Herr Schleinitz of
Leipzig, for whose birthday on October 1st Mendelssohn had
composed *Nachtlied,* his last composition before his death.

Jenny Lind, in carrying out her loving plan, invited her artist
friends to assist her in a grand performance of *Elijah* at Exeter

Hall, on Friday, December 15. *The Times* for December 16, 1848, reported :

"The grand performance of the Oratorio of *Elijah,* in aid of the 'Mendelssohn Foundation for Free Scholarships in the Leipzig Musical Conservatory', took place last night. Exeter Hall was filled, in every part, by one of the most brilliant and fashionable audiences ever assembled in a public edifice. . . .

"The performance last night was complete and splendid. The vocal and instrumental arrangements, under the able and zealous direction of Mr. [Julius] Benedict, were on a very grand scale. . . .

"But it was in the fine Air in B minor, *Hear ye, Israel,* which opens the second part, that Mademoiselle Lind first had occasion to put forth her entire strength. So grandly did she deliver the Allegro—*Thus saith the Lord; Be not afraid*—that the decorum which the audience had with difficulty observed during the first part was unanimously thrown aside, and applause burst from every part of the hall. The ice once broken, enthusiasm became the order of the day. . . . The high E and G with which the opening phrase [of the Quartet] begins were attacked with wonderful firmness, and sustained with full and brilliant quality. The shake upon D sharp that finished the second phrase was deliciously even and in tune. In short, the whole was as near perfection as is compatible with human fallibility, and may be pronounced Mademoiselle Lind's most successful effort during the evening. . . .

"Altogether, the performance was worthy of the cause for which it was instituted, and a considerable sum will be devoted, by its means, to the advancement of the Mendelssohn Foundation at Leipzig."

In summing up, Holland and Rockstro say : "Until the end of her life, Madame Goldschmidt continued to take the deepest interest in the Foundation, and the election of its Scholars; and we cannot doubt that her name will be remembered, in connection with the Memorial she raised to her departed friend, for many a century to come—for the Foundation is legally secured, and remains in perpetuity."

Between December 4, 1848, and February 2, 1849, Jenny Lind gave seven concerts for charitable purposes—five hospitals, the Mendelssohn scholarships, and the orchestra which accompanied her on her provincial tour. Together with the receipts from the concert for the Brompton Hospital, the sum which she thus raised reached the astonishing total of over £10,000.

On April 3, 1849, a performance of *The Creation* was announced for presentation at Exeter Hall, in aid of five more important charities.

Jenny Lind's fervent wish to retire from the operatic stage was evident in conversation and correspondence with her closer friends. Her resolve was a bitter disappointment to the public and to Mr. Lumley, who had counted on her for the whole season of 1849. When his theatre fell into financial difficulties as the result of losing his main attraction, she came to his rescue and promised to sing six more operas in concert form. But the public was not yet ready for such purely musical experiences, and her first presentation turned out to be a financial failure. As a result of this, she unselfishly put aside her personal aversion to fully staged performances and consented to continue as usual for the remaining five operas. The last of these, *Roberto il Diavolo,* which took place on May 10, 1849, before the Queen, the Court, and an enthusiastic audience, was her farewell to opera after eleven active years. Now at last, having done this great favour for Lumley, she was free to leave the stage for ever.

Jenny Lind had made many fast friends in England, and this must have been a factor in her choice of this country, long afterwards, as the place to retire to. There were the Grotes, whose home was open to Mendelssohn, Chopin, Thalberg, Lablache and others. George Grote, the historian of Greece, was in close contact with the chief writers and thinkers of the day—John Stuart Mill, Cornewall Lewis, Milman and Sydney Smith. Mrs. Grote's brother and sister meant much to Jenny Lind through the years. As we have seen, the Bishop of Norwich and his wife, Mrs. Stanley, served as temporary substitutes for the loving and motherly Amalia Wichmann in Berlin. Their daughter, Mary Stanley, became devoted to Jenny Lind for life, and the non-musical Arthur turned out to be a close friend of the Goldschmidts in England until his death at Westminster in 1881. Mrs. Stanley exchanged long and frequent letters with

La *Figlia del Reggimento*: representation in metal and cloth

Worcester candle snuffer (1848) known as "Diffidence", showing Jenny Lind as the Swedish Nightingale

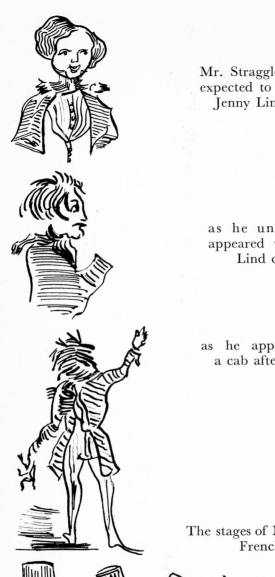

Mr. Straggles, as he was expected to appear when Jenny Lind came on

as he unexpectedly appeared when Jenny Lind came on

as he appeared calling a cab after the opera

The stages of Mr. Straggle's French hat

Cartoon in the *Illustrated London News* showing the fate of one enthusiast at Her Majesty's Theatre on the night of Jenny Lind's London début

her sister, Mrs. Augustus Hare, on the subject of Jenny Lind. Others, including the Queen herself, were lastingly attached to Jenny.

Through the Grote connections Jenny Lind met a distant relative of theirs, a young captain in the Indian army, Claudius Harris, who was visiting Joseph Grote's home in Newcastle. Captain Harris seemed completely overcome by the charms of the singer, for he could never have imagined that a young woman associated with the stage should have retained the goodness, perhaps even the naïveté, of the charming Jenny. During her tour of the provinces he followed her about like a schoolboy, to Edinburgh, Glasgow and Dublin. On her part she had felt him to be a "dull young man", but later on she softened this estimate because of their common ground in religious interests.

Finally Jenny sang at Bath, which was Captain Harris's home city. While she was there she called on his mother and sister and asked after him. As soon as Harris heard of this he rushed to Bath from Mrs. Grote's cottage at Burnham Beeches. There he saw Jenny frequently, and ardently began to press his attentions on her. Jenny Lind asked him to confide in his mother about their plans for an engagement, and he confessed that he had already done so, much to her gratification.

However, a dark cloud floated over their relationship. Both mother and son, adhering to the strict Evangelical system which considered the stage to be utterly incompatible with their religious life, insisted that Jenny Lind should cut herself off from the stage by an official statement to that effect in the marriage agreement. The mother detested the very thought of actors and actresses. True, Jenny Lind herself had found the conditions of theatrical life intolerable. But it was another matter altogether to have the moral rectitude of her entire past career challenged by the Harrises. Moreover, she felt an absolute conviction that she must have the power to make her own engagements and control her earnings—this not for any selfish reasons but because she considered the administration of the money earned for charity a sacred trust. In Captain Harris's view, it was contrary to the scriptures that a wife should have this freedom.

On May 10th Mrs. Grote left for Paris, where she stayed at the Maison Fenci, in the Champs Elysées, hoping that Jenny

Lind would find the time to rest with her there. One night, some days later, she was sitting before the fire, nursing a headache and wondering about her friend, when there was a tap on the door. It was Jenny, who confided that the engagement was at an end. She had finally realized that it would be impossible for her to be tied to such a demanding mother and son.

The two had long walks in the Tuileries and drives in the Bois de Boulogne. There was the opportunity to call on Meyerbeer, and every morning Jenny Lind gave a singing lesson to Miss Ebeling, a Swedish girl. Her old friend, Madame Arnemann of Hamburg, appeared in Paris at this time.

But happiness was soon at an end. The great singer, Madame Catalani, who was an old friend of Jenny's, was found dead in her bedroom, stricken with cholera. The Republicans were threatening an uprising because of the intervention of France in Italian affairs, and Paris was in a state of siege. Jenny Lind and her entourage fled to Amiens, together with her guardian, Judge Munthe, who had arrived from Stockholm for consultation and advice.

A letter to Amalia tells much of her feelings at this time:

XXVII
Schlangenbad, July 11, 1849

Really I could write volumes! But it is just this that makes me dislike writing so much—that, in point of fact, one can convey so little by it! I have gone through a great deal lately, my dearest Amalia, and long from my innermost heart to tell you about it; but not to put it all down on paper . . . Things and experiences touched me which deeply affected my peace of mind. Everything in my innermost heart was undecided for a long time. I did not know what to write. I was very near to marrying. But again it came to nothing; and I believe this was for the best, for there were things that did not please me, and probably I should not have been happy . . .

Oh dear! I am myself again: and I feel that I have many other duties, and great duties, to fulfil towards others—though

the finest, the most sacred of all—I mean, a mother's love, is
forbidden—nay! denied to me!

I have often wished for the blessing of motherhood, for it
would have given me a much-needed focal point for my affec-
tions. With it, and through the varied experiences that accompany it, I could perhaps have achieved something better than
that which I have attained up to now.

But dearest soul! I am happy all the same! Inexpressibly
happy : for have I not been favoured by fate with much more
than I deserve, such as is vouchsafed to few here on earth . . . !

I left London for Paris, where I tumbled into the most fearful
cholera epidemic. Thither my dear guardian came, in order that
I might have someone trusty near me. Then on June 13 we
went to Brussels, and from there to Cologne, and have looked at
the Rhine. Old father Rhine! how glorious it is, and ever will
be! Well, I had meanwhile sent my Swedish lady to London to
pack up; and to have my things sent to Sweden. But one day
I went to see a renowned doctor at Coblenz, to consult him
about my shattered nerves. He examined my head, and also my
heart (which are both terribly fatigued), and then told me that
unless I nursed myself properly, I should probably have a complete breakdown when I took up work again. He has forbidden
me absolutely to sing for six or eight months : and has sent me
here for a fortnight, in preparation for four weeks at Ems. After
Ems I am free until after October. But I wish to spend next
winter in Sweden, where I have many matters to arrange.

Dear, kind Amalia! could not we meet somewhere? Are
you not in need of Ems? Could we not go to Switzerland? . . .
or shall I come to Berlin or will you come to Ems? or are we
not to meet at all???? I have just received a letter from London, confirming the news of —————— ————'s reappearance! I am
much surprised at this. May a gracious God preserve me from
such a calamity as to come before the public as an old lady!
Rather bread and water! While in Paris, I saw Meyerbeer and
his new opera. I was glad to see him again, for he has always
been very good to me : but I prefer his earlier operas.

Will you please remember me to old Frau Beer? And how
is dear Professor Werder? Has he completely forgotten me? And

old Frau Schroeder?[30] I love a person like that immensely! I
know nothing more beautiful than such a faithful old being,
going about in a family, who really lives only in taking interest
in what concerns her master's family, and in feeling for them
and with them! Greet this dear old soul; and also good Nanke:
and Frederic.[31] It was my happiest time when every day I saw
all this before me! If I send no greetings to my Professor, or my
beloved brothers, it is because this goes without saying. Everything that I have written to you in this letter is also meant for
the father and his sons. God protect you all!

Send a friendly answer, and then I shall know that you *never*
could have doubted that I remain for ever and ever,

Your faithful, and sincerely loving,

Jenny Lind

Jenny Lind proceeded to carry out her doctor's orders for a
"grape-cure" at Merano in the Tyrol. She had set her heart on
having the Wichmanns visit her and had sent a note to Amalia
(according to Holland and Rockstro, Vol. II, p. 355), the exact
date of which is not known, saying, "You must not put your-
selves out, dearest, but it would be delicious if you did resolve
to come to Merano." The plan was that Jenny would be there
from the middle of September to the middle of October.

Our collection of letters reveals that she sent Amalia a letter
from Ems about the possible visit:

XXVIII

Ems, August 28, 1849

Beloved Amalia:

I am so alarmed that you are all angry with me now because,
out of kindness to me, you have changed your plans again. God
knows better than anybody that I did not want to act without
the proper delicacy, and now I am also very uneasy because
of my letter to Rudolph at that time.

---

[30] The porter's wife at the Wichmanns' house.
[31] The manservant.

Perhaps I did something then that displeased you, and this hurts me more than I can say. Nevertheless, I can assure you, dear Amalia, that nothing bad was meant by it, and I hope you know me well enough to realize that I should be very deeply unhappy if I had done anything displeasing to you. Forgive me if, without my knowledge, this should be the case. I simply thought that after your first letter we could just as well have made a part of the journey together—for my destination in any case is Merano.

On the sixth of September I must go to Frankfurt. From there I shall take the train direct to Basle, because I should like to see a little bit of Switzerland, and I beg you, therefore, definitely not to expect me in Innsbruck. We shan't see each other until we are in Merano. For I am not coming to Innsbruck and secondly, I do not know just when I could get there. You do understand me, dearest, don't you? We shall see each other again in Merano, if God wishes it, and you will not wait for me to join you in Innsbruck.

Thus, about the eleventh or twelfth of September, I shall probably be with you in Merano. Please don't be angry with me, and greet our father and brother very heartily.

From your
deeply loving
Jenny Lind

(P.S.) Should you now want to change your plans, please do so for Heaven's sake, without regard to me, and don't, I implore you, let me be the cause of your doing anything you are not satisfied with!

Finally the Wichmanns did join Jenny Lind, settling with her at Ober-Mais, a village just above Merano. Offers followed the singer there, including one for concerts in America. But for the moment all were ignored, as this was a time for rest.

The whole party returned together in October, via Vorarlberg, to Frankfurt. There Jenny Lind separated from her dear Wichmanns, leaving for Hamburg, where she had agreed to sing at some concerts.

A letter, full of deep feeling, was despatched from Hamburg.

XXIX

Hamburg, October 29, 1849

My own dearest Amalia:

I was greatly overcome when you were all gone! I am, of course, accustomed to being alone; but I knit myself too quickly to people whom I love, and cannot believe that I must lose them again! I had got so used to enjoying the happiness of your companionship, which always does me so much good, and of seeing your domestic love, that I was sad the whole of Sunday! You dear good people! To think that you should allow me to share your happiness! You cannot think how grateful I am for all this, dearest!

While at Hamburg Jenny Lind received a summons from the King of Prussia, Frederick William IV, who had given her the title of Court Singer in 1847, asking her to come to Berlin to sing to him and his Queen on the latter's birthday. The message was sent from Count Redern via the Wichmanns.

XXX

I cannot tell you how deeply your letter touched me! It cannot but move my very heart to think that His Majesty the King should be so gracious to me, and I shall account it the greatest joy if I can succeed in giving even the slightest pleasure to the Queen by my singing . . .

Pray tell Count Redern that I gladly obey the King's desire, and will be in Berlin by the 19th of this month [November].

Ah! dear Amalia, I long for you all! It is still true that it is with you, and yours, that I have spent the happiest days of my life!

During November and December, 1849, she sang in several concerts at Hamburg. At one of them, in the Grosse Tonhalle on November 22, Otto Goldschmidt played a piano concerto. He also accompanied her in two other concerts. The memory of Mendelssohn was a strong bond between Otto and Jenny. At last she had undertaken to sing once again those songs which had lain dormant within her for a period of two years. Jenny was so impressed with Otto's gifts, and especially with his dedication to Mendelssohn's music, that two years later she turned to him quite naturally, during her American tour, when the unexpected return to Europe of Julius Benedict left her without an accompanist.

Taubert was sent to take Jenny Lind back to Berlin, and she was quite delighted at the idea of seeing the distinguished Hof-Kapellmeister. According to Holland and Rockstro (vol. II, p. 357) she wrote to Amalia the day before:

"I cannot help laughing with joy when I think of seeing that dear man Taubert tomorrow. I confess that it gives me immense pleasure!"

In Berlin, she was happily installed as usual in the home of the Wichmanns.

Earlier, Herr Berg had been sent by King Oscar I of Sweden to try to persuade her to sing on the occasion of the marriage of the Crown Prince Charles (later King Charles XV), planned for the Spring of 1850. After meeting her in Hamburg, he was disappointed to hear of her decision to give up singing in opera; however, she did promise to sing in several concerts during 1850. Moreover, she accompanied her old singing master back to Lübeck, and remained there for a while, as she explains in the letter which follows:

XXXI

December 7, 1849. Lübeck

Dearest Amalia:

I write to you in no very bright spirits, for I have no chance of seeing you and yours again as soon as I had hoped. My good Josephina has fallen ill. It is nothing dangerous, thank God! On the contrary the doctor thinks that, after it is over, she may be better than she was before.

But you will understand that I cannot, and will not, leave her. So I shall not be able to be with you, my dear ones, by Christmas Eve, but must wait for the New Year to knock at your door... Ah! write me a few words before that, dearest, and say that you still think kindly of me, and how it goes with all of you.

Your grateful and loving

J. L.

At this time she was torn between offers from Russia and America, but on January 8th, 1850, she writes a short line to Madame Wichmann (Holland and Rockstro, Vol. II, p. 364):

"I am not to go to Russia after all, for Russia is thrown into the background by another big plan. But I shall come to you as was planned at first, even though for only a short time."

The great American showman, P. T. Barnum, had sent his agent, J. H. Wilton, to Europe to propose to Jenny Lind that she should come to America to sing under his management and at his expense. In the Hotel du Nord, Lübeck, with no other companion but Mlle. Ahmansson, the singer trusted her own judgement to the extent of signing an agreement for the big tour. It was thought, however, by those closest to her at the period, that she had consulted Judge Munthe before taking the decisive step. At the same time she seems not to have informed the Wichmanns of the full details of this plan at the time of signing the contract.

Julius Benedict was secured as pianist; a famous baritone, Giovanni Belletti, was particularly chosen by Jenny Lind instead of the customary tenor.

Jenny agreed to sing at one hundred and fifty concerts, including oratorios, within the period of a year, or at most eighteen months, with the express stipulation that she should in no case have to appear in opera. All travelling expenses and hotels for herself, a lady companion and a secretary were to be paid, and Jenny was to be allowed a maid, a servant and a carriage and pair, with a fee of $1,000.00 (£200) for each concert or oratorio in which she sang. Other provisos, favourable to Jenny, were worked out by Mr. Barnum and his agent. She had, for example, the right to terminate the tour after sixty concerts, and again after a hundred concerts, with appropriate penalties. Here was a wonderful chance to continue her work without pressure for a return to opera.

From Lübeck she wrote to Amalia Wichmann about all this:

XXXII

Hotel du Nord, Lübeck, January 12, 1850

Beloved Amalia!

I now wish to give you a clear idea of my future plans, so that you—and all yours—may know the truth and be able to distinguish the facts from mere reports.

I have decided to go to America. The offer was very brilliant, and everything was arranged so nicely that I should have been wrong to decline it; and since I have no greater wish than to make a large amount of money in order to found schools in Sweden, I cannot help looking upon this journey to America as a gracious answer to my prayer to Heaven!

In the course of one or two years I shall be able to earn there a very large fortune, and after three years should not need to sing a note unless I wished to do so. I felt in my heart that I should not go to England at the present time. Indeed, sometimes I am very sad and I often have to fight my pessimistic moods. But now I feel quite relieved, for I signed the contract only three days ago, and thus I can dismiss England from my mind—for the time being. Herr Benedict (son of the M. Benedict whom you saw at Merano) comes with me, and you could not meet with a more honourable man or better friend and at the same time a more reliable musician. An old friend of mine, Signor Belletti, goes also. He is a distinguished singer, and we have known one another for twelve years, dating back to the old times in Sweden. In short, nothing could have been arranged more admirably. I at once gave up any plans for Russia, and did so gladly; for Josephine could not have stood a Russian journey . . . So now we remain—and more particularly Josephine—in Lübeck until we take the first steamer leaving for Stockholm, which I hope will be in April. Then I go home—sing there a few times in concerts, as I have promised my King to do, make arrangements in view of my long absence from Sweden, and leave Stockholm again on the last day of June or the beginning of July, in order to take a "milk cure" somewhere (only not too far away). This I must have concluded by the middle of August in order to leave for Liverpool, there to take the steamer for America early in September! It would be soothing and strengthening to my feelings, if I could pass the latter weeks of my stay in Europe

in your company, my beloved friends. There is no need for me
to say any more about how happy I should be if this were possible. I should much like to go to Salzburg! But more of this
when we meet at Berlin; for I fancy I shall come to you at
about the end of February or the beginning of March. I shall
probably spend some days in Hanover soon, in order to sing for
the good Crown Prince; I have been urged to go there so much
that I mean to comply with the request.

Well! I hope that now I have told you something about us,
and you know also that we are not going to Sweden this winter.
Greet my beloved, revered father! Greet the brothers also, and
the good Schröder! When shall I receive the letter from her?
How good it was of Herrmann to write to me! and how clearly
do I see the scene on Christmas eve in your home! We had a
Christmas tree too! The good people here are fond of us. Next
Thursday, the 17th, I am giving—a concert, you think? Nay, a
children's ball! and I look forward to it with a right royal joy!

Farewell, beloved soul. Preserve to me your inestimable love,
as I remain for life

Your ever grateful and loving

Jenny

"The good Schröder" in the above letter was the great singer
Schroeder-Devrient, a friend of both Jenny Lind and Mendelssohn.

Otto Goldschmidt came over from Hamburg to be present
for the children's ball, and it is recorded that he danced with
Jenny Lind many times. She had a passion for dancing, but
often denied herself the pleasure of it for the sake of her voice.

She sang on February 9th at Hanover for the benefit of the
poor, then at Oldenburg on the 12th, and at Bremen on the
20th. She sang again for charity at Hanover on the 25th, and
at Brunswick on the 27th. During this period she refused
several offers from Berlin which were so generous that she termed
them "shameless".

The trip to America was vividly in her mind at this time, as
this letter to Amalia shows:

XXXIII

Hanover, February 14, 1850

Dearest Amalia :

You write to me so kindly, but I don't know how I am supposed to take it all, for I simply cannot imagine that my uninteresting self pleases you so much, and that you long for me as much as you say that you do. But I know that you are always an angel of kindness towards me.

I shall not sing in Lübeck until I am back there again, and Josephine of course will stay there until we go to Sweden.

I well know the goodwill of Herr von Küstner,[32] and am grateful from my very heart; but indeed I could not dream of accepting such shameless terms from Berlin : and I cannot in any circumstances entertain his kind proposals. I request you, my dearest, to tell him this as coming from me. I can only stay a very short time in Berlin; I cannot help this. And I shall only sing twice—once for an institution for the poor, as I have already promised Frau Alexander Mendelssohn, and once (but this is between ourselves) for poor Herr Hendrichs,[33] who has been so ill, and has lost so much money because of it; after that, I sing no more. I have so much to think of about America. And then, I cannot leave my Josephine alone too long !

This is my answer ! I am in such a hurry that I scarcely know what I am writing. But I do know this, that I love all of you eternally and will remain my life long,

Your loving and grateful
Jenny

A few days later another letter was sent :

XXXIV

Hanover, February 23, 1850

Dearest, you must not be angry with me for having to write

[32] Herr C. Th. von Kustner, General-Intendant der Königlichen Schauspiele between 1842 and 1851, of whose kindness and support, while she was in Berlin, Jenny Lind always spoke with much warmth and gratitude.
[33] An actor at Berlin in whom Jenny Lind took much interest.

to you that I cannot get to Berlin until Wednesday of next week.

I am hunted and harried like a poor hare. But after all, everywhere I enjoy nothing but great friendliness, so that I should indeed be thankless if I were not satisfied in spite of all the bother. I have also had to put off a concert on account of a severe headache, and am therefore two days later than I meant to be.

On Tuesday evening I am singing in Brunswick, and on Wednesday I shall be with all of you.

Don't be cross with me, but continue as always to love me.

Your
Jenny

On the way to Berlin Jenny stopped in Brunswick for a concert there, receiving as usual the highest possible praise.

Early in March she found herself happily settled in the home so dear to her, in Berlin, in the old room crowded with early associations. The Wichmanns, their servants, porters, etc., were completely devoted to Jenny Lind; their feelings amounted to little less than worship.

Professor Jungken, a famous physician attached to the Court of Berlin, wrote to Professor van Jaeger in Vienna such a delightful account of Jenny Lind that we should like to digress in order to quote a few passages:

"For a month the town was all agog for the arrival of Jenny Lind. For a month the Wichmanns had engaged her rooms; at last, she appeared! We saw her first at a brilliant soirée at Count Redern's, which all the royalties now in Berlin honoured with their presence . . .

"Two days after this we heard her at a concert. She is, certainly, a marvellous apparition, with an attraction that is irresistible. Her voice is very beautiful; her delivery is noble; but her play of expression!—that is positively bewitching. She will sing no more on the stage; but, then, there lies in her eyes, in her mien, an expressiveness which is equal to the most perfect acting. It is a delight indeed to listen to her; but a still greater delight to *see* her sing. Her delivery of her songs is, undoubtedly, unsurpassable, and it is peculiarly her own . . .

"A day before her departure, Madame Wichmann was good enough to ask us to tea alone with the Lind. For a couple of hours she charmed us in the highest possible degree, and we found out what a really delightful and dear child she is. I had to tell her everything about your family, your fortunes, your affairs—she insisted on knowing it all."

Jenny's plans took her to Dresden, again to Berlin, and finally to Hamburg, where she wanted to help the Schumanns at their concerts. Her arrival took them somewhat by surprise. She offered immediately to sing at Clara Schumann's concert in Altona, the adjoining city to Hamburg. Clara and Robert Schumann were enchanted with her, as always, for she sang his songs to perfection, and her very presence meant an overflowing audience.

Late in March Jenny arrived in Lübeck to find Mlle. Josephine Ahmansson much better in health. In a letter to Amalia Wichmann she reports on her arrival :

XXXV

Lübeck, March 26, 1850

My little dog, too, was so affectionate, jumped up at once on to my lap, and lay there as quiet as possible ! Just think, dearest, that I sang twice in Altona and Hamburg ! The Wieck-Schumanns were there, and they were delightful, and too remarkable and gifted not to kindle love and admiration. And I count it a special honour to have been allowed to sing a couple of little songs at their concerts.

[A bracelet had arrived through the Lord Chamberlain, from Berlin, as a tribute to her singing. She goes on :]

And it cannot but be a great pleasure that their Majesties should have personally chosen the gift. But my singing has always received such appreciation and reward that it was a kind of recreation to be allowed just once to sing without recompense on an occasion like that. But kings, and queens, and such like must always put a high value on their pleasures !

On April 10th, 1850, she wrote to her good friend, Baroness French, that her plans now were to take the boat for Sweden in about two weeks. She would remain in her native country until

about the end of June; after that, she would go to Schlangenbad and Ems; from there to London for a stay of only a few
days; and then on to Liverpool for the start of her trip to
America.

Jenny reached Stockholm on May 12th, aboard her old friend
the steamer *Gauthiod,* delayed a bit at the start of the voyage
because of ice. She was to sing at six concerts in the Royal
Theatre at the end of May and the beginning of June. Also,
there were to be two state concerts in June honouring the wedding of the Crown Prince.

In June she received a tribute from her native people which
touched her deeply. A medal was struck in her honour, sub-
scribed to by almost every person of distinction in Sweden, beginning with the King. The tribute addressed to her ran as follows:

"To Jenny Lind: the lovers of music at Stockholm have,
during the present spring, as well as during the winter season of
1847-48, enjoyed a succession of memorable feasts, at which
they have admired alike the Artist's genius, and the nobility of
heart wherewith she has dedicated her triumphs exclusively to
Charity and Benevolence, and has thereby testified that the aim
of true Art is something higher than to please, and to astonish.

"Having been privileged to witness these festivals of Art,
where the beauty of the soul found its expression through the
medium of song, the lovers and friends of music are desirous that
the great artist, on leaving her native country, should carry
away with her some outward token of this period of her life,
of which the inner memory, which is at all times the companion
of virtue, will follow her through life, until that other world is
unveiled to her of which she has been the messenger to us
through the language of music.

"The undersigned have received the agreeable charge of
handing to her this simple souvenir."

The medal was struck separately in gold, silver and bronze.
On the front was the bust of Jenny Lind, while on the back
appeared the figures of Charity and Patriotism, standing on either
side of the Genius of Song.

Jenny Lind left her country on June 27th, planning to
fill a few engagements on her way across Europe before join-
ing Benedict and Belletti, who awaited her in London.

She sang at Bremen on July 4th, at a concert given for the benefit of Carl Reinecke, Kapellmeister and pianist, for whom she always cherished a warm admiration. After that she remained in Schlangenbad, gathering strength for the coming American tour. From there she wrote to Amalia Wichmann:

XXXVI

Schlangenbad, July 9, 1850

Beloved Amalia :

I have been here for three days now, and hasten to let you know this. What are you all doing this summer? Shall I have a chance to see you or not? Please forgive me for not having let you know about this sooner; up till now I have been rather uncertain about my own plans for the summer, because I left Sweden so late. I shall stay here until the eighth or ninth of August, and then I shall go direct to England and America. On August 21st I sail from Liverpool.

I don't need to add what a pleasure it would give me to see you, but I fear that you must already have made your plans for the summer. Is it possible that you might come to the Rhine after all? In that case, let me know whether I ought to reserve rooms here, for everywhere is full this year. But compared with other places it is still quiet. Our good doctor from Lübeck, Dr. Heyland, has just arrived with his wife and daughter, and they are such lovable people.

Let me hear from you soon!

I hope that things are going well with you, my dearest, as they are with me. I am feeling very strong, and so is my good Josephine.

I kiss and embrace you all, and pray to God for your happiness.

Your loving
Jenny

On August 6th she sang at a concert in Baden-Baden for the benefit of the horn player Vivier, a friend of Julius Benedict. Then she travelled through England, staying in London only two nights, after which she went to Crumpsall, near Manchester, the home of her dear friends the Salis Schwabes. There she rested for a few days before fulfilling her engagements at Liverpool on August 16th and 19th. The Schwabes accompanied her there, so that she felt the intimacy of close friendship. Jenny Lind had planned to sing the *Messiah* on August 19th for the first time, this concert being a forerunner of those of later years when she proved herself an unequalled interpreter of the work. "I Know That My Redeemer Liveth" has become a byword for Jenny Lind until this day.

"The depth and sublimity of the music exhibited Mlle. Lind's talents in a totally new light," writes a critic in Liverpool who was present at the performance of the *Messiah*.

On August 21st Jenny left Liverpool on the steamer *Atlantic*. Because of the intense excitement expected before the departure, the local authorities took extra precautions. She boarded the steamer much earlier than the time of sailing, and her carriage followed a route through little known streets. The surging crowd had to content itself with a sight of Jenny waving a handkerchief from the paddle-box as the vessel took leave.

Upon her arrival in New York, the same intense excitement prevailed. Finally, Barnum was able to place the "Nightingale" in his own carriage, after which they set off for Irving House. Barnum gives this account in his memoirs, written years afterwards : [34]

"Within ten minutes after our arrival at the Irving House, not less than twenty thousand persons had congregated around the entrance in Broadway, nor was the number diminished before nine o'clock in the evening."

Castle Garden was the scene of Jenny's first triumph in America, the details of which, along with an account of her great tour, have filled a small volume and have provided much material describing this phase of her career. [35]

[34] *Struggles and Triumphs, or Forty Years' Recollections of P. T. Barnum.* Written by himself. Author's Edition, The Courier Company, Buffalo, 1875 edition.

[35] See *Jenny Lind in America* by C. G. Rosenberg, published by Stringer & Townsend, 222 Broadway, New York, 1851.

Rosenberg's little book on the American tour, published more than a

This is what she wrote to Amalia Wichmann :

XXXVII

Philadelphia, December 5, 1850

My dearly beloved Amalia :

I feel such a great desire to write you a few lines, my dear Amalia, that I cannot keep silence any longer. I long to know how you all are; and should like, too, to tell you something about myself; for I know how great an interest you take in my fate, and that you wish also to know how I am faring. I will no longer restrain myself; for I find my thoughts flying to you with such love and confidence that I feel grateful and happy in the mere act of communing in spirit with you. And I know you have not forgotten me!

What are they doing in Germany? I am very anxious about the situation there. Will there really be war, Amalia? If so, where will you go? For God's sake, write me a line about this, so that I shall know what you intend to do in case events should get beyond your control.

If all goes ill in Europe you might come to America, and fetch me home. How is Otto? Is he stronger by now? I was so glad to see him in Baden-Baden; and fancied that in him I saw you all.

I and all of us are extremely well. My head is quite recovered; and my voice is better than ever. The climate here is very good. Nearly the whole of the autumn we have had a clear blue sky, such as we had at Merano, when it was at its best. And we shan't have any winter this year because now we are going to the South. At the beginning of January we plan to arrive in Havannah [sic]. My address after that still remains "Jenny Lind, care off [sic] P. T. *Barnum*, Esqre, American

---

hundred years ago, is charming but all too brief. The tour is something that merits much fuller treatment; and it has never been presented in all its detail, in our opinion, simply because no one has carried out the necessary research. But there are many fascinating details waiting to be discovered and presented to the public.

Museum, *New York*. In this way letters will always reach me safely (but write also : *via Liverpool*). Mr. Barnum behaves extremely well towards me : and I could not wish for anything better.

In July we hope to be back in Europe again, for we hope to see the Great Exhibition. Ah ! if *you* were to come there ! You have never been in London, Amalia; how interesting it would be to see it ! Think it over, dearest !

If you see Taubert, tell him, please, that they will not listen to anything here but his song "I must be singing". Since I have got a very good translation of it in English, I have to sing it at *every* concert. Greetings to all my friends—Herr Taubert, Professor Werder, Magnus, Madame Mendelssohn, etc.

How curious the customs here are at times ! The women over here—how strange they are sometimes ! I shall have many things to tell you when I get back.

I wept for joy the other day when the Prussian Envoy, Herr von Gerolt, brought us greetings from Her Majesty the Queen of Prussia. When next you meet His Excellency Herr von Redern, pray tell him how truly grateful I feel for this mark of Her Majesty's sympathy. Many greetings to him, too, our Count, Herr *Bookish,* director of Linné's, Frau Kunde, Fräulein Tactor and *Herr Jahn.*

Faithful love to you all !

From yours ever gratefully,

Jenny

(On the side of the letter appears :) My Josephine sends all good wishes from an overflowing heart.

Copies of old *New York Herald* newspapers, on our desk as this manuscript is prepared, give accounts of Jenny's concerts at Castle Garden and Tripler Hall, beginning at the time of her arrival in New York in September, 1850. Later issues, and in particular that of December 19, 1850, speak of her visit to President Fillmore's family in the White House on December 15, a visit which preceded the grand Southern tour that was about to be undertaken.

The trip took the Lind entourage to Richmond, Wilmington (N.C.), and on down to Charleston, where they spent Christ-

mas Day and celebrated New Year's Eve. The party then departed by steamer for Havana; went from there to New Orleans;
and then up the Mississippi with concerts in Natchez, Memphis,
St. Louis, Nashville, Louisville and Cincinnati, and on back east
to Pittsburgh, Philadelphia and New York.

Jenny Lind's mother died shortly after the American adven-
ture began. Although mother and daughter had never been very
close to each other, Jenny quite understandably grieved over the
event, for during the past few years their relationship had become considerably more affectionate than before.

Once again in New York, an important event in the singer's
life took place: the arrival of Otto Goldschmidt from Germany. He had come to replace Julius Benedict, who found it
necessary to return to Europe for health and personal reasons. At
Jenny Lind's suggestion, Otto was occasionally billed as a piano
soloist in her concerts. His lengthy classical solos were probably
a boring obstacle for the public that had come to hear Jenny
sing. He was, therefore, not very popular either with his captive
audiences or with Barnum, who, however, conceded that Otto
was "a very quiet, inoffensive gentleman, and an accomplished
musician".

Jenny had a number of reasons for wishing to terminate her
contract with Barnum before fulfilling the minimum of one hundred concerts. It was inevitable, with two such dissimilar personalities, that there should come a parting of the ways. Everything considered, however, Jenny's personal relationships with
Barnum, who was always pleasant and correct, were remarkably friendly and untroubled.

In the first place, Jenny's manager and others in her group
were constantly trying to persuade her to break with Barnum.
Their reasons may have been acceptable enough, but their under-
lying motives were basically selfish. This situation kept Jenny
constantly in an atmosphere of backstage intrigue.

Secondly, Jenny felt a natural aversion to the spectacular and
vulgar publicity with which her concerts were constantly publi-
cized. Barnum exploited all his extraordinary powers of show-
manship in presenting her to the American public, and there
must have been times when she felt on a par with other

protegés of his like Tom Thumb or the Bearded Woman of Genoa.

Thirdly, she probably found most distasteful of all the high price of the concert tickets and the manner in which a gullible public was regularly induced to pay exorbitant prices for seats through preliminary auctions by Barnum's agents. For example, Barnum himself records that Colonel William C. Ross bid $650.00 for a ticket in Providence, while in both Boston and Philadelphia top bids came to $625.00. In almost every city many tickets, through changing hands, reached a sum several times higher than the fixed price.

Moreover, there was little doubt that the tour had proved to be physically exhausting and that Jenny must have felt some anxiety over the resulting strain on her voice. For the past nine months, under contract to Barnum, she had sung an average of one public concert every three days under every imaginable condition and in geographical areas requiring long journeys often made with primitive means of transport.[36]

It was only natural that she should desire to escape from this demanding schedule and should long to become her own boss. She therefore notified Barnum in a formal letter of her desire to forfeit after her ninety-third concert the sums agreed upon in her contract under him. This forfeiture amounted to a total of $32,000, as follows :

(1) $7,000, i.e. $1,000 per concert, for the seven unsung concerts;

(2) $25,000 which she forfeited on the understanding that, should she cease at the hundredth concert instead of reaching a possible top number of one hundred and twenty five concerts, she would owe for each such concert one thousand dollars.

Even after these deductions had been made, Jenny's share of the undertaking amounted to $176,000, and, allowing for her

[36] Jenny Lind sang a total of 95 concerts for Barnum from her first appearance in New York on September 11, 1850, to the termination of her contract with him, ending with the concert of June 9, 1851, in Philadelphia. Of this number, however, only 93 concerts were actually under the contract, since she had sung two concerts before the contract took effect.

habitual generosity to charities[37] and other worthy causes in America, there still remained in her possession a sum large enough to provide her and her family with financial stability to the end of their lives.

A further example of her scrupulousness in financial matters is revealed in the charming letter which Jenny had written to Otto Goldschmidt's father on the occasion of her engaging his son for the American tour. The Library of Congress has been good enough to allow us to use this letter, recently acquired by them. It shows how careful she was in making sure that the financial arrangements were to the benefit of her new accompanist, and her anxiety that her future father-in-law should be at ease in the matter.

New York, August 4, 1851

My Dear Sir:

I hope you will have the goodness to excuse me if I take the liberty of burdening you with a few lines, although I write your German language so badly. Since, however, every word on my part originates only from the purest sympathy for your son, I know I may depend with complete confidence upon your kind indulgence.

You will certainly understand that I must make my situation completely clear to you. Since you do not know me well enough to be sure whether or not my choice of your son has been made with the utmost sincerity, and since it is difficult for me to speak with him concerning money matters—for it seems to me that both of us are timid in speaking of such things—therefore it is all the more important for me to know that the contents of this letter are brought to your attention.

I have sung so much during these last ten months that it is now absolutely necessary for me to rest for several weeks. It is my intention, however, to give more concerts in America later

---

[37] In New York alone the amount set aside for charity amounted to $15,000, and in nine of the other cities which Jenny Lind visited she gave $35,000 for this purpose. In addition to the more than $50,000 thus accounted for, there were many other private charities which were not officially listed.

on, and in making these plans I have taken into consideration the fact that, since Herr Otto G[oldschmidt] has made the long voyage over here, it would perhaps not be quite right if he returned immediately to Europe without having accomplished very much. I should like, therefore, to propose to him that he should work with me in any future concerts in this country, especially as I am absolutely convinced that it would be much better for his health if he rested here for two months and bathed in the ocean, instead of letting himself be plagued by the good people of Hamburg and having his fine, rich spirit depressed by giving piano lessons. Herr Otto G. has accepted my proposal, and therefore he is not returning home this autumn. I hope and wish that in this matter I have not acted against your wishes, since I understood in the letter from you and your wife that you would have nothing against my keeping Herr Otto a little longer in America. Moreover, you will doubtless often have realized that he has such a clear insight into everything, and is always guided accurately by such a right and noble feeling, that one must respect his judgment. For the concerts at which Otto has worked with me up to now, I have put out at interest here in America the amount of 25,000 Marks, since one can do this with money in America very *safely* and advantageously. He will not need to withdraw any part of this sum, for it remains in good hands until, as we hope, the amount has multiplied itself many times, and also because Herr Otto will have much more to do in the coming concerts than has been the case until now. Be assured, dear Sir, that I shall always treat your son with generosity, all the more so because money has little charm for me, and then only when I can use it for the benefit of my fellow man.

It will give me great happiness if I have been able to put you at ease concerning a number of things, for I understand very well how close to the heart of his parents the fate of such a person must lie.

Please deign to accept the assurance of the highest esteem of your

Faithful
Jenny Lind

Soon Jenny was depending so much on Otto Goldschmidt for

sympathy and advice that a deep feeling arose between them, ending in their marriage at Boston on February 5, 1852. The wedding took place in the home of Dr. and Mrs. Sam Grey Ward. Dr. Ward was a banker in Boston, and the agent there of Baring Bros., London. Bishop Wainwright, of the Episcopal Church, officiated. The couple left for Northampton for a brief honeymoon.

We are grateful to the New York Historical Society for permission to quote a letter in the Westervelt collection which Jenny wrote in English, and which gives an intimate glimpse of her feelings about her husband some weeks after the marriage. We reproduce it exactly as Jenny wrote it.

Northampton (Massachusetts), March 30, 1852
My dear Dr. Baird :

Accept my most heartfelt thanks for the very kind letter you have written to me.

I ought to feel greatly ashamed for not having told you myself anything of my being married, but I know how troubled you are with so many peoples affairs that I feel as if I would not add to your *labour*.

I feel most thankful towards my Heavenly Father that I in all truth can say that I gained the best, most disinterested friend in my beloved husband—he is so mild and kind-hearted, that it is only seldom you will find a similar character. We are both musical souls—and we feel in all matters the greatest, most perfect sympathy I can imagine.

He is younger than me, as you may perhaps know—this certainly had been better was it not so—but, his youth exists more in his face than in his soul, for really he is as stady as an old man, that is to say—a stady old man ! My husband's soul is open for Religion and every noble sentiment. I feel great esteem for his manner of thinking ! Excuse me for writing so much about him, but I flatter myself that you have not unwillingly listened to my naration. We thank you very much for your kind invitation to your house. Excuse that it will not be possible for us to accept the same, as we only intend to make a very short stay in New York.

I send hereby *five* of my autographs, as you said that *five*
Ladys were wishing for them!—With my kindest regard to Mrs.
Baird and our mutual greeting to yourself I remain dear Dr.
Baird

Yours ever truly

Jenny Goldschmidt

late

Jenny Lind

P.S. My best thanks for the book you so kindly have sent me.

Once free from Barnum's contract and now managing her
own affairs, Jenny found considerable relief from the pressures
and strains of the earlier tour. She could spare her voice whenever necessary, and could travel at a more leisurely pace. But
a price had to be paid for this new independence. Jenny's
manager, a young Scot, Charles Seyton, and her secretary, Max
Hjortzberg, were far from being the equal of Barnum's highly
trained staff. And without Barnum's blatant spotlight focused
upon her, Jenny found it somewhat difficult to attract the
crowds which she had formerly drawn. Smaller audiences and
mounting running expenses meant less money, which in turn
entailed the abandonment of orchestral accompaniment and the
curtailing of her more spectacular songs. Her image as a benefi-
cent angel therefore began to pale somewhat. And her insistence
that her husband should share the stage with her, not only as
her able accompanist but also as her artistic peer, alienated some
of the music critics and emboldened them to cast aspersions
upon her singing and to criticize this most generous of women
for profiteering. By the time Jenny had sung at forty concerts
in seventeen different towns, both she and Otto were ready to
call it quits. They went to New York City in May, staying in
Delmonico's and giving three farewell concerts—on May 18 and
21 at the Metropolitan Hall, and again at Castle Garden on
May 24. Five days later they left New York on the steamer
Atlantic once again. The grand tour of America had at last
come to an end, and, in spite of its anti-climactic close, Jenny
nevertheless departed with two outstanding acquisitions: a considerable fortune and a husband who was, to quote Barnum,
"an accomplished musician".

PART II

"WE, THEREFORE, LEAVE her company at this point, parting with her just at the very summit of her career as 'Jenny Lind', leaving her still moving forward into continual triumph, at the top of her force, in the fullest exercise of her powers—leaving her to pass out of our sight, under the low happy doors of home, into the quiet and the secrecy of wedded life."

The above statement was printed in Holland and Rockstro at the end of their account of Jenny Lind's career. Part II of this present work now takes up where they left off.

These later letters to Amalia Wichmann reveal an intimate picture of Jenny Lind's married life, and are rich in details concerning her relationship with her husband and her children. Many of them are suffused with a warm glow of marital happiness and motherly affection.

Indeed, it was just this state of domestic contentment that Jenny had longed for throughout all the previous years of her career. As early as 1838, when she was eighteen years old, she had been strongly attracted to Julius Günther, a young tenor who sang the leading roles with her in the Stockholm opera. This relationship, however, came to nothing when Jenny, always wise and restrained in affairs of the heart, realized that the young man apparently did not reciprocate her admiration. After this little romantic flurry, she kept a firm control over her emotions. And yet the dream of a home and family of her own still haunted her, and at times seemed almost more important than her career.

Later, as we have seen, a handsome young army officer, Captain Claudius Harris, became so enamoured of her that she stood this time on the brink of marriage. This too came to nothing, and the parting seemed to end her chances of ever becoming a wife and mother. With stoic resolution she abandoned her hopes for marriage and steeled herself for a life of artistic performance. But this pessimism proved unfounded, as the following letters, filled with the praise of Otto, of her home, and later of her children, establish.

After their return to Europe from America, in the spring of 1852, the couple stayed at Fenton's Hotel in St. James's Street, and Otto was introduced to Jenny's many friends. The remainder of the summer was spent on pleasure trips in Switzerland and at Scheveningen. Otto Goldschmidt took the trouble to learn Swedish, and eventually he made trips to Sweden to consult with old Judge Munthe on Jenny Lind's business affairs.

In the autumn of 1852 they settled in Dresden, where they were destined to remain for five years. During this period a son, Walter Otto, and a daughter, Jenny, were born to them. They were in constant touch with many German friends, as well as with their numerous English friends. Jenny continued her artistic career, singing in oratorio and interpreting the music of Mendelssohn and Schumann.

In the latter part of the year she wrote to Amalia:

XXXVIII

Dresden, December 13, 1852

My Beloved Amalia:

The impressive invitation has arrived safely and caused us great amusement. You are so extraordinarily good to us that we simply don't know what to say. It would give us the greatest pleasure to spend Christmas in Berlin with you, but we must forego this pleasure since we can't arrange our affairs so that we can leave our house now.

Such a visit is all the more impossible because the concert for the Gustav Adolph Club (in Berlin) will not take place until about the end of January. If we also went to Berlin for Christmas, that would mean three visits there. I really am *terribly* sorry, but I must ask you *not* to expect us, for we cannot come. A thousand thanks for the kindness which you have once again shown me through your enduring friendship for me, and the kind welcome which you yourself, and all of you, have granted to my little husband ! ! He asks me to express his thanks to you and the others, and he regrets as much as I do that we shan't be able to enjoy your *tea* and *Pyramids* on the 24th of this month.

But we are still hoping that your Herrmann will give us the great pleasure of a visit, and I implore your kind support of this proposal, that is, if you can dispense with his company for several days. It would be so nice if he would visit us. We could invite him to better music than the quartet-playing at your house! We have rooms in the floor above us which are ready to receive our guest, although they are neither comfortable nor inviting. But unfortunately at the present moment we haven't anything else to offer. Otto and I are counting upon Herr Herrmann's visit to us.

Beloved Amalia, Otto would like to send the enclosed letter to Herr Joachim, who is arriving in Berlin about this time. Otto doesn't know where Joachim will be staying, and therefore asks Herr Herrmann to be so good as to deliver the letter to him—for Otto thinks that Herr Herrmann will surely be getting in touch with him. In my opinion Joachim is the greatest artist now living.

Many greetings and much love from
Your most loving and thankful
Jenny
(On the side of her letter :) Josephine sends many greetings. She would like so much to be going to Berlin.

Joachim had studied under Mendelssohn in Leipzig as a fellow pupil with Otto, so it was natural that Otto should want to get in touch with him in Berlin. Otto had left for that city before the next letter was written, and of course he planned to stay with the Wichmanns.

XXXIX

February 11, 1853, Dresden
Most Beloved Amalia :

May I ask you to be so kind as to give the enclosed letter to Otto, if he is in Berlin? If, however, he has gone to Hamburg,

then please, sweet Amalia, have your maid take it to the Post
Office immediately.

You are quite right in thinking that it has cost me a great
deal not to be able to sing at the Gustav Adolph function and
not to see all you dear friends. But I feel it is better for me to live
quite calmly here, since I *cannot* sing without great agitation,
and this is just the thing that has the worst effect on my head
and fatigued nerves.

I hear that my good Otto was so very warmly and hospitably
received by you, dear parents, and that you have invited him to
stay at your house with you dear people. I am very grateful to
you. He is sweet and good, and deserves every kindness. But
please do not do anything out of kindness to both of us which
could be burdensome to you. It would not be right for you to
do this.

Will Otto bring Herrmann with him to Dresden, perhaps, or
can't you let him go, you dear egotistical mother? Herr Herrmann would hear some good music here, and a little change
wouldn't do him any harm. Please think it over and kiss my
father for me, and tell everybody, too, that I shall love you all
forever with unchanged devotion.

Your
Jenny

A few days later another letter is despatched to Amalia con-
taining, right at the end, a piece of momentous news:

XL

Dresden, February 25, 1853

My Beloved Amalia:

Thank you for your lines which I received this morning. I
can't repeat often enough how happy it makes me that you and
father are so kind to my Otto. I am not allowing myself even
to imagine that you are inconveniencing yourself in the slightest
degree for his sake, for then there would be no pleasure either
for you or for him, if you intend him to stay with you during
his visit to Berlin. Apart from this I like the plan very much in-

deed and am very happy about it, since I know how lonely and uncomfortable he would feel in a hotel. Otto will probably arrive at your house on Wednesday.

And now here comes my big, shameless request to you, dear Amalia. I urgently ask you to have the instrument which you are so kindly placing at Otto's disposal tuned frequently in advance (don't be angry with me) so that it will accord perfectly with the orchestra. Sometimes pianos are too high or too low for the orchestra, and often, when they have to be retuned in a hurry, the instrument suffers or does not retain its new pitch in the concert hall. So, sweetest Amalia, please ask your tuner to come on Monday so as to check the condition of your piano.

What has Herr von Berg done now? You have made me very concerned about him. I should be very sorry if he is the victim of a stupid, womanish trick. He always appeared to be so good and sensitive. I am very curious to learn how he is faring in the circumstances.

The day before yesterday a gentleman is supposed to have called at our house (actually we were not at home) who said that he came from Berlin and knew "Professor Wichmann". I thought it must have been Herr Herrman, but we haven't been able to find his name in any newspaper. It would certainly be a great pleasure if Herr Herrmann were to come, but I am hoping that in the spring you, father and Herr Herrmann will visit us, since we have rented a very big house in quite an attractive neighbourhood, and move into it at the beginning of April. I should like so much to see you and the rest of the family this summer, for perhaps this is my last spring on this earth! But keep this between us. I probably don't need to say more?

God bless you all. Kiss my beloved father on the mouth for me. I genuinely feel as if I belonged to your family. God protect you all.

Your true,
Jenny

Poor Jenny felt that the trials of having a baby would be too much for her, which accounts for her believing that her time on earth was drawing to a close!

Another letter follows not long afterwards :

XLI

Dresden, March 15, 1853

My Most Beloved :

I must express to you in a few words my heartfelt thanks for the wonderful, loving hospitality which you have shown to my dear Otto. I am deeply moved that *he* too has won a place in your friendship, and you can certainly imagine quite clearly what a true feeling of joy this creates in my heart, for every day I love my sweet Otto more deeply and steadfastly because of his great kindness and his faithfulness to me. And you will understand completely what a great joy it is to be devoted to one's husband. That you, Amalia, love him as a *person* is naturally of greater value to me than the fact that you also esteem him somewhat as an artist. I should like to say, too, how much pleasure you gave me by your offer of your house for the afternoon concert, since I knew in advance that Otto would win much more recognition in this way than he would in a concert hall, where often so many things can disturb one, as was presumably the case with the orchestra.

Otto has undertaken all this for me because he wants, for my sake much more than for his own, to make not too bad an impression in Berlin.

But nevertheless I see, my dear Amalia, how much his presence disturbed your house, and I am sorry, although I know so well from my own experience how reluctant you are, with your tact and kindness, to admit it.

Now you are going to see Rudolph, and I am quite delighted on your account. Is his little wife still well? And you must come to see me when everything is happily and successfully over at Rudolph's, and you have settled down again after the first joyful tidings.

Then you and father and as many of you as I can have will attend the *baptism*. You have already promised Otto this, and before you come I wish that you and father would send a blessing through the air for the sweet little creature which is now stirring within me and awakening into life—and, if it should grow up without a mother, give it a loving glance from time to time! Tell father this from me.

Oh! I feel so profoundly and deeply happy, and I go to my

This photograph was probably taken during one of Jenny
Lind's early visits to London. Reproduced by kind permission
of Lady Welby

View at Exeter Hall (*Illustrated London News*)

fate with peace in my heart. Whether it be life or death, God
will take care of the child as He has taken care of me, and I trust
confidently in His eternal mercy. I simply say, His Will be done!
I am very—in fact exceptionally—healthy. I have felt so little
unpleasantness during these past four and a half months that
I can hardly believe it. Oh, dearest Amalia, can anybody describe one's joy when the child stirs within one? No, it is too
wonderful. When I write this you can see my love for you, for
otherwise I am very shy about expressing my feelings. But you
will certainly not misunderstand me.

Thank my dear father and Herr Herrmann on my behalf.
I will pray to God for them. This is the only way I can show
my love for them at present. Farewell. Greetings to Rudolph
from your always loving and thankful

Jenny

(P.S.) There's probably not much more to hope for with regard
to the Mendelssohn project.

P.S. Oh, sweet Amalia, please send me if you can the two criticisms of the Gustaf Adolph concert. Otto says they are sure
to be in the same newspaper from which you sent me the others.
Please don't be angry with me.

(Along the side of the letter appears:) How sorry I am about
Herr von Berg.

As the time grew nearer, she went on to write Amalia in
June:

XLII

Wackerbarthsruhe, near Dresden, June 2, 1853

Dear Amalia:

You good, sweet person! Thank you for the darling, beautiful
baby cap! How happy I was that you have already thought
of my child in so charming a manner. I believe, however, that
you think the little third member of our family is already here?
Actually, you know, the catastrophe will probably not take place
until the end of next month. If I should survive the event, and
if I am still *living* at the time of the baptism, then it is likely

that the ceremony cannot take place before the end of August. You must all arrange matters so that you can visit us, even if you have to come later. Unfortunately I have to return to town for the crucial time, since the doctor will not allow me to have the child out here in the country.

It is really magnificent here. The whole thing will be difficult in the heat of the city. My Amalia, the first thing for you to do is to look after your health and then come to visit us when you can. In any case, we can't decide anything more definite for the moment. It is still fine here in October. Perhaps you would all come in the autumn? Meanwhile, I am grateful anyway that you want to come. But, I repeat, come you *must!* After all, I must have something too to gladden my *heart*. It has been so long since I have seen any of those whom I love!

I am *very healthy*. Of course, a little bit cumbersome, but on the other hand remarkably carefree. I have not felt so well for years.

I simply love your baby cap; this little gift expresses so much friendship from you, dear Amalia. I am so happy to be bearing a child and to experience its sweet awakening!

A thousand greetings to Rudolph and his wife. May God grant her His blessing. Kiss father on his forehead. My regards to Otto when you write to him. My sisterly greetings to Herr Herrmann. And be assured that I love you very, very much. I hope that we can arrange matters so that you and father can be here for the baptism.

Your true and grateful
Jenny

P.S. Herr von Berg will always be welcome.

Jenny was grateful in the autumn to be able to write the following letter:

XLIII
Wackerbarthsruhe, near Dresden, September 13, 1853
Dear Amalia:
With a thankful heart I have now progressed so far that once more I can lead a completely active life; and now one of my

first duties is to send a word to my dear parents (for I still love
you very very much) to tell them that my beloved child
and I are getting along magnificently and that up to the present
everything has gone so much as I would wish it that all I can do
is simply to thank God in silence—words just don't suffice at
all. Also, I wanted to say how glad I am about Rudolph's happiness. What satisfaction it must give him to press his little
son to his heart. I am longing to meet his dear wife—my dear
sister! I hope that Rudolph is now completely recovered. I am
very sorry to hear that he was sick, especially at a time when he
needed all his strength to support and help his wife.

How are you feeling, dear Amalia? I should like to know exactly how your health is, but you *never* go into details about
it. My voice is just the same. I haven't felt fatigued in the
slightest, and, like the lady of whom you spoke, I too must
say, "Is this the thing that women moan over so much?" This
is, of course, unreasonable, but I certainly must not omit to say
that it is certainly quite different if this whole important matter
does not take place naturally and normally.

I do not know yet what we shall do for the winter. I am nursing my child, and this is my first and most important duty.
But of course both Otto and I are longing for our art and our
sphere of artistic activity, as useful citizens of the community,
and I would never have believed how very deeply I am devoted
to my voice and to my art. I now say that the greatest good on
this earth that exists for me, after my love for God and the
one He sent to us, the greatest good is my child, my husband,
and my voice.

Otto has gone to the Tyrol for several weeks. This was very
necessary for him—that good, noble person who has done so
much for me and who bears such a heavy burden.

He has now left to you the decision whether or not you and
father come here for our child's baptism—if you can possibly
manage it. I mustn't beg too much, because I know that it won't
be very easy from the point of view of your health to make the
trip here. But I will ask, nevertheless, and knock at your door,
dear friends, to find out if it will be possible for you to give us
the joy of your presence on the sixth of October.[38] But you are to

[38] Jenny Lind's thirty-third birthday.

be completely free in your decision, and whatever answer my
Amalia may give me, whether yes or no, I shall always read
your goodness into it, and know that if you do not come you
will nevertheless still remain our good friends. If my beloved
Amalia would be so good as to let me know as soon as possible
whether you are all coming or not, then if you are not coming
I could think of someone else before it is too late.

Please write to *Wackerbarthsruhe, Niederlässnitz,* bei *Dresden.*

Warmest greetings to father and to all of you from your
faithful and thankful

Jenny

Apparently this letter was an enclosure in the following one
sent to Rudolph on the same date :

XLIV

Wackerbarthsruhe, September 13, 1853

My dear good Rudolph :

I live in the pleasant hope that you have not forgotten your
old sister Jenny, from Sweden, and therefore I cannot refrain
from sending you, most esteemed brother, my deepest and most
sincere congratulations upon the great joy that is yours : that
of pressing a healthy child to your fatherly heart. And of course
nobody can understand this happiness better than a happy
mother, which I have now become, you know. God gives us His
strength to bring up our children in the right way, and lead
them by our own example along the path of virtue and true religion. This is a noble, difficult task, but love will help us to
achieve it.

I hope, my dear Rudolph, that you are completely well again
and that your chest is strong and healthy. It always seemed to
me whenever I *grasped* you in my arms as if you were made of
pure iron and steel. But you must have caught a cold, and since
there are *so many things* for the master of the house to take
care of you must be very cautious and not expose yourself to
any draft.

I am really delighted that your dear wife has come through everything so well, and I hope that you will express my most heartfelt greetings to your helpmate.

If your parents have already left Litschen, I beg you to be so good as to forward the enclosed letter to them as soon as possible.

Farewell, my dear good Rudolph. Stay healthy and happy, and that God may protect you all from pain and danger is the prayer to Heaven of your always loyal, loving sister—

Jenny Goldschmidt
née Lind

Soon another letter was despatched to Amalia:

XLV

Dresden, September 23, 1853

Dear Amalia:

I am very happy that you all intend to give us the great pleasure of coming here, and it is of course a wonderful added pleasure that Herr Herrmann is coming with you. Otto met Herrmann in Merano.

I just hope that the weather will stay as wonderful as it is now. We have a big house, and yet I scarcely dare invite you three because so few bedrooms in the whole house can be used on account of the dampness. In the summer it was all right, but now it is autumn.

Meanwhile, if my Amalia, after she has seen the house, still wants to stay with us, then that would be delightful, and just what we should like. But in any case please let us know *when* you are coming, so that I can meet you at the station (as you always did with me). Don't rob me of this pleasure even though you will have to submit to the boring task of writing once more. Welcome! A thousand times welcome! If the weather stays as fine as it is now, it will almost be as beautiful here as in *Merano!*

Your
Jenny G. L.

About two months later, Jenny was thinking of Christmas, and so she wrote to Amalia early in December :

XLVI

Dresden, December 7, 1853

Beloved Amalia :

I think the time is now here when I might ask you, in all seriousness, whether you would like to come and spend Christmas with us. I hope I don't have to tell you how genuinely welcome you are.

What is father doing? Is his head better? In any case, I think it would be better for you two to come here, since you would otherwise be alone in Berlin, for neither Rudolph nor Otto can be with you there.

We have a friendly house, fresh air always at hand, and the big garden here offers magnificent walks even in winter. We have three rooms which, although they are on the fourth floor, are completely at your disposal—if you should decide to stay under the same roof with us—an arrangement which I certainly think would be the most convenient for father.

Herr Benedict is probably coming too.

I am not speaking with a mother's partiality when I say that our baby is really a good, sweet child, who I believe will give you pleasure too. He now gets gruel twice a day, and thus you see, my dear Amalia, that I have not completely disregarded your good advice.

Now, please make up your mind to come, my Amalia. Do let me know that you are coming—which will give us a home-like, old fashioned Christmas. I appeal to you from the heart, and it is the same with Otto. Welcome! And I rejoice at the thought of gazing once again into the face of my father and *mother!*

God be with you.
Your loving
Jenny

Early in the year 1854 Jenny and Otto Goldschmidt were able

to return to their artistic career together, and during this time
they were on tour in Berlin, Leipzig, Vienna and Pest. As we
know, her repertoire now consisted exclusively of lieder, oratorios
and isolated arias from opera. But if Jenny felt any longing to
return to the operatic stages of these cities, in which she had
been so much applauded, her letters do not reveal the fact, and
indeed it is clear, from everything she wrote and said in later
life, that she was deeply thankful no longer to be subjected to
the demands of opera, which took so much out of her. Otto,
being the good businessman that he was, made himself respon-
sible for arranging the business details of such plans. He accompanied her, as well as conducting and playing solo at many concerts. The following letter reflects a part of such activities :

XLVII

Dresden, February 6, 1854

Dear Amalia :

A thousand thanks for your invitation, as always so gracious,
to stay at your home. You know that you and your family make
Berlin like home for me, and that your house will always be like
the home of my parents. But—I have firmly decided that you
should not have all this noise in your house any longer because
of us. So we shall stay at a hotel. But I will come to visit you
as many times and as often as I can and as you want me to, and
that's the way things will stay! Moreover, dear Amalia, since
we intend to give several concerts [in Berlin] the trip into
town would certainly be a bit lengthy, and for Otto it would be
difficult to arrange everything from a distant place like Teilner
street.

I am leaving my Walter here, even though this will be hard
for me; still, it is my duty to think of the comfort of the child
rather than my own wishes. And, of course, Josephine will be
staying with him, and so I am leaving him in the very best
hands. I think that in this way I have arranged everything in
the best possible manner.

I have just finished weaning him. I have been working at it

for two months, little by little. He is now completely adjusted to it, and thank Heaven everything has up to now run smoothly, although *I* am not very *comfortable* in the process. However, I am not suffering any pain, and all the rest is of course unimportant in comparison. I'll tell you more about all this when we can talk.

I am deeply sorry that father has had his headaches again. Lucky Otto, to be in Rome!

I feel certain that Mme. Arnemann is alone. Oh, she is a lost and shattered creature! The poor woman has had horrible misfortune with her children. Just imagine—two of the others are also consumptive.

Dear Amalia, don't try to change our decision about staying at the hotel, for we are firmly resolved to stick by the plans that I have just outlined.

I kiss and embrace you and father, and remain in good times and in bad ones

Your thankful and loving

Jenny

P.S. My husband sends you his most cordial greetings through me.

A few days afterwards Jenny wrote again :

XLVIII

Leipzig, February 14, 1854

My Beloved Amalia :

I am sorry to give you the trouble, but I must impose upon your goodness and ask you to reserve a couple of rooms for me at the Hotel du Nord (wasn't that the name of the hotel where Otto and I stayed in December, 1852?). I need only a bedroom for myself, in which my maid can also sleep, and a little reception room. For I am coming alone for the first week because Otto has to go to Vienna. It doesn't matter what floor the rooms are on, so long as I have quiet and don't notice any tobacco smoke. I should also like to have a servant's room. I will come on Monday, the 20th, and will stay until the following Monday.

Sweet Amalia ["Amalienchen"], do try to engage the two rooms for me, and don't bother to let me know if you can't reserve them at the Hotel du Nord, but reserve them somewhere else in the neighbourhood. It's all the same to us.

I am singing here today. My dear baby is . . .[39]

Another letter followed:

XLIX

Dresden, February 17, 1854

Beloved Amalia:

I had been back from Leipzig only a couple of hours when I found your dear note, and although it may be quite shameless of me, I simply cannot bring myself to renounce the pleasure of staying at your house. For to be at the hotel in Berlin without Otto and Walter would certainly be hard. If I were only sure that you would not be inconvenienced by my acceptance, I should terribly much like to be with you all. Give me *one room*. I can honestly reassure you that it will be quite sufficient for me, since my maid is very respectable and can very well sleep in the same room with me. Don't worry about any servant at all if I stay at your house, for then he will look out for himself in any case.

And now I make one more request, and this is a serious one: do *not* meet me at the *station*. I am not sure when I shall arrive, and in any case I would much rather have my first greetings at your house.

Please don't be angry with me for making such claims upon your kindness once more. It is a real consolation to my heart that I have not been able to refuse your invitation. Please forgive this imposition of your loving and always thankful,

Jenny

P.S. Please tell Herr Herrmann for me that the Eye-talian words match the Mazourkas (mazurkas) very well.

[39] The remainder of the letter is lost or has been destroyed.

The letter that follows, almost three months later, expresses clearly the lasting friendship between Jenny and Amalia:

L

Vienna, May 4, 1854

Dearly Beloved Amalia:

Your sweet, kind words of the 30th April reached me yesterday in Hünden (?), and if I hadn't had a concert yesterday you would have received an answer immediately. Forgive me, dear Amalia, for not writing for so long; it was certainly not my intention to seem to want to bear you any *ill will*. Who indeed has more deserved my friendship and love than you—who, from the very first moment of our friendship, have continued to show me only the most touching sympathy—indeed, I dare to say, love? So please do not believe that it entered my head for one moment to think that you might want to hurt me, or that you could ever misunderstand my intention about the dress. No! No! Only when Otto came back from Berlin and told me that he thought you had taken my little joke about the dress amiss, and had seemed to suggest that you thought I had wanted by this means to "half pay" for our stay at your house—then, I confess, I was very upset. But not for long, because I knew my Amalia, and realized that she certainly knows that no pecuniary remuneration, no type of dress, not even the richest in gold, silver and precious stones, could repay your dear friendship. Once again it's almost comical that you could have such little confidence in our finances as to believe that I could not spend 54 *Pr. Th.*[40] without upsetting our bank balance! This attitude seemed very peculiar to me too, for, praise be to God, our resources are more than adequate.

Dear Amalia, the whole matter of the dress boils down simply to this: when you first sent me that other old dress in the hotel as a joke, and when I saw how worn out it was, so much so that you couldn't possibly wear it again for any decent occasion —then I felt such an intense joy that I didn't want to deprive myself of somehow getting another dress for you, in the hope of

[40] Prussian Thaler.

soon seeing this one as worn as the other, *only to be replaced again by a new one* from me. You see how far I would go! Only the Lord knows when we shall see each other again. Maybe not for years. The thought that in this intervening period you will now and then wear a dress from me makes me very happy, because it seems to me nice to wear apparel which one has received from a person on whom one depends. Therefore, I am continuing to wear this Indian scarf (as a jacket) which you gave me, and also the black lace scarf that you gave me recently in Dresden. I thank you, my sweet Amalia, that you have kept the dress. I did not believe or expect that you would do anything else. But it nevertheless gives me so much pleasure to be sure of it now. May the Almighty bestow happy and healthy days upon my Amalia in that dress!

We are well. My beloved Walter is beginning to say "Ta-ta, Pa-pa, fu-fu" and this simply enchants me. *It is too charming!*[41]

The local doctor whom we asked also said I must go to Kissingen. Our concerts have been excellent, but now it is beginning to get hot. We shall leave Vienna about the end of May. May God keep my Walter healthy!

I kiss my dear father's hand and forehead! You I embrace with my whole heart, and pray that God will keep and protect all your loved ones for you. For all my life I remain

Your true loving and thankful,

Jenny

LI

Kissingen, August 11, 1854

Dear Amalia:

How dreadful to learn that you are ill again. I wish that I could help you, and also learn more about your condition. Do you have everything that you need, and a good doctor? I don't want to bother you for long.

Thank you a thousand times for the book, so beautiful in every respect, which you gave to my dear child. I hope it will

[41] Jenny wrote these four words in English.

accompany him throughout his life. Only I should like to have had your and father's names in it, but you can inscribe this little token of love for me when—God willing—we see one another again.

We are all well. I feel better, and Walter is in splendid health. He has two teeth and his little legs are beginning to get strong. Goldschmidt and Josephine are going with the child to Dresden, and I go to Norderney for four weeks. The separation will be very difficult for me, but it is best for Walter's welfare that he should live quietly.

I am expecting my father from Sweden, who will go with me to Norderney.

Taubert was here for a day, together with his oldest daughter, and it gave me real pleasure to see his face again. Whenever I see someone from our former circle, I also see all of you and am carried back to those happy days again.

Perhaps I have already plagued you too long. Please don't be angry with me. I should like so very, very much to hear soon just how you are.

Dear, good Rudolph. Write me a few words to put my mind at ease. Otto, Walter and Josephine send all of you many greetings.

Your ever loving and thankful,
Jenny G.

Jenny was at Norderney at the same time as the King and Queen of Hanover, and a warm friendship developed. Jenny went on riding trips with the King, and joined the royal couple for supper, after which she and the Queen sometimes sang duets together. In her memoirs, the Queen recorded how memorable Jenny's presence and warm personality made their stay. She would tell them stories of her past life, often springing up and going to the piano to play and sing. The Queen wrote: "Her singing at that time was more full of soul, if possible, than at other times." They all returned to Hanover together, and as they were sailing over the North Sea to Bremen Jenny was so overcome by the loveliness of the scene around that she burst into songs. "We were all completely electrified by the overpowering impression," the Queen wrote, "and the tears ran down from my dear husband's eyes."

In this letter Jenny mentioned her father for the first time to Amalia. He came, according to plan, to Norderney to join his daughter. Mr. Lind continued to live a few more years in Sweden, making occasional visits to the Otto Goldschmidts in Germany.

It may be unnecessary to point out that the "Otto" mentioned in the first paragraph of the following letter is Otto Wichmann, whereas in the second paragraph the reference is to Otto Goldschmidt.

LII

Dresden, January 10, 1855

Dear Amalia :

I wonder if I shall get two letters from you before you receive one from me? I always have so little time in which to write. I simply cannot tell you how sorry I was not to find you in Berlin upon my return from Sweden, and how astonished I was to learn that you had undertaken a trip to Italy. But when I heard about Otto's condition then, of course, the riddle was solved.

We were both very, very sorry when we heard that the two of you passed through Dresden and didn't let Otto and our child come to see you. But time after time I have enjoyed so many kindnesses from all of you that I shall never believe you would not accept a few kindnesses from me and mine—especially since I have now received two letters from you (one from Brünn), while up to now you haven't had even one from me. But I have followed you in my thoughts, you may be sure of that.

Your letter today has inspired me with a great desire to spend a winter in Rome soon. I have a deep and true longing to go there. I *know* that I should be happy in Rome. After this winter we must do something to improve our bank account; otherwise time will get the better of us. We are planning, therefore, to make a little artistic tour in Germany and perhaps in *Holland*. We shall leave the child here with Josephine, and when the spring comes, God willing, we shall go straight to some beautiful spot and later to Switzerland, and then probably next winter to Rome. Please arrange things so that you and yours will be there too. That would be just wonderful.

Walter is very strong, thank the Lord, and gives us endless pleasure. We are all well and I feel much, much stronger. My dear Otto is also well. We didn't stop at all in Berlin, and thus saw none of our acquaintances there. I simply hurried to Zurich to my beloved child after going through storms and danger on the trip to Sweden. Our Christmas brought us roses, too—to Walter's cheeks! The child was radiant. He was given a rocking horse, and that was really fun.

My voice is still the same, and this makes me beside myself with joy! Oh, *mon Dieu,* when I think what I might be able to do with it!—But, my dear good brother Otto, what do you mean by being sick? Take very good care of yourself and pray to the Lord, and he will make you well again. Kiss my dear father on the mouth and forehead for me. I am as happy as a child that you are well situated and are breathing the divine, healing air of Italy. Please go back there next winter, and until then God protect all of you and watch over you in all your comings and goings.

Loving greetings from all of us except Walter, and from him a kiss on the hand through

Your loving and thankful,
Jenny

Whether or not Jenny's voice was "still the same" is a matter for conjecture. There were critics who thought that it had lost its brilliant technique during her eighteen months' absence from the concert stage at the time when her first child was born. Yet the voice retained much of its unique power to ravish the listener. For example, Carl Shurz, who heard her in 1854, wrote his impressions of her singing in *McClure's Magazine:*

"She was no longer young when I heard her. Her appearance, though still exceedingly pleasing, had become somewhat matronly. Her voice might perhaps not have retained all of its original birdsong-like lightness of warble. But there was still that half-veiled tone, as if there were something mysterious behind it;

that velvety timbre, that strange magnetic vibration, the mere
sound of which could draw tears to the eyes of the listener. Of
all the great voices I have heard, and I have heard many, none
was so angelic and went so entrancingly, so caressingly, to the
heart as Jenny Lind's." And during the 1854 tour a Berlin critic
wrote : "Jenny Lind-Goldschmidt is the musical demon of the
century : to fight against such a power is a futile effort for any
other artist."[42]

During the early part of the year 1855 Jenny sang in concerts
in Hamburg and Bremen, while from March to May she was
engaged in Holland, singing at Amsterdam, Rotterdam, Leyden,
Utrecht, the Hague, Haarlem, Dortrecht and Friesland. It was
the first time she had been to Holland, and the tour was bril-
liantly successful. In June she sang at the Lower Rhine Festival
at Düsseldorf, repeating her visit in the years 1863 and 1866.
Other distinguished musicians who were there included Joachim,
Liszt, Brahms and Gounod. The Norwegian composer Halfdan
Kjerulf was amazed that, though world famous, she was yet so
simple and unaffected, taking part in every rehearsal, and always
singing with absolute care and tirelessness.

LIII

Dresden, May 12, 1855

Dear Amalia :

Upon my return from Sweden yesterday I received your dear
lines of April 21st, and I must laugh at your eagerness
about our future concert in *Rome*. When you talked about it
so much in the letter before last I thought you were joking. But
since you now refer to it so much again I must tell you, dear
good Amalia, that in the first place we don't know whether we
shall go to Rome next winter, and that, if we do go there, we
haven't the *slightest intention* of devoting our time in that city
to concert activities. We don't want to spoil our beautiful visit
to Rome with all that. I hope my good Amalia has not spoken
publicly about this.

We are now going to the Rhine with our child. I am singing

[42] *Jenny Lind* by Joan Bulman, p. 291.

in a music festival in Düsseldorf on the 27th, 28th and 29th of
this month, and afterwards I shall go on to Bad Ems so that
Walter can enjoy the mild air there, while Goldschmidt will go
to Sweden in June. In July we shall all go to Kissingen and then
to Schneitz in the *Tyrol*.

Walter is quite well. He is walking beautifully. In addition
to a couple of jaw teeth he has a mouth full of pearls. He gives
us a lot of pleasure. We grown-up, big people are all well,
although somewhat worn out from so much travelling during
the last three months.

I am glad to learn that father hasn't had any headaches. May
God protect you all and keep you from evil as much as He deems
right for you. Maybe we shall meet somewhere during the
summer. Until then, fare thee well, dear Amalia.

I remain your true and thankful
                    Jenny G.

By this time, Otto Goldschmidt was assuming the burden of
financial arrangements which had plagued Jenny before her
marriage. In fact, in another five years she cancelled the pre-
nuptial contract in which she had reserved for herself the disposition of funds accumulated during the American tour, thus
giving him complete control of the money matters of the Goldschmidts. In time, Otto also assumed the duties of the aging
Judge Munthe and took over the management of the various
Lind scholarships and charities in Sweden. The old Judge remained their close friend to the end of his days. Otto visited
Sweden in the spring of 1855 in order to meet his wife's guardian
and familiarize himself with her financial affairs.

LIV

                                   Kissingen, August 9, 1855
Dear Amalia :

I have just received your dear lines of the first of the month.
It appears from your letters as if you had already written to me
about our meeting in Rome. But I have not received any such
letter. Your last letters to me were from Rome. I am so sorry

that we did not know when you came through Vevey and Basel,
and so forth. Now I scarcely know whether we shall find each
other. We stay here until about the 22nd of August, and we
haven't yet definitely decided whether we shall go to *Vevey* or
Tegernsee.

Otherwise we are well. Walter is very gay and lively. Josephine was very ill here, but she is well again now. How glad
I am that you are all well.

I often saw Frau v. Rosenberg in Ems. She was so very
lonely, which made me very sorry for her. But I think somebody
is going to have to give her a *shaking up*[43] and a *jolt*. She seems
to be so terribly blasé. She didn't even speak of her husband
once.

Please forgive my handwriting. We are returning to Dresden
for the winter.

Aufwiedersehen there or in Berlin. Many greetings from
your

Jenny G.

A few days later this note was sent :

LV

Kissingen, August 15, 1855

Beloved Amalia :

Through Mr. Buttner I have learned that we shall have the
pleasure of meeting you and father, since you are stopping in
Soden. Therefore I want to ask you whether you will be there
next Wednesday, the 22nd of this month, and further whether
we could visit you in Soden. If so, perhaps you will leave word
at "The Roman Emperor" for me, telling me where you are
staying and whether you can perhaps come to Frankfurt that
day?

I am looking forward very much to seeing you in the flesh
once more, and therefore Auf Wiedersehen ! A kiss to father
from your

Jenny G.

[43] Jenny Lind wrote "sütteln" here for "schütteln".

The letter given below was sent to Amalia only eight days
before the Goldschmidts were the centre of attraction at a musical
evening at Windsor Castle, where they appeared before the
Queen and Court. No other performers were present, except
for the orchestra, which Otto directed. Jenny sang Haydn's "On
Mighty Pens", Otto's own arrangement of Chopin's mazurkas
for the voice, a song by Mendelssohn, and then Taubert's
"Cradle Song". The eventful evening inaugurated a great winter
tour of fifty-two concerts in England and Scotland between December, 1855, and June, 1856. The *Creation,* the *Messiah,* and
Elijah were the oratorios given, along with other miscellaneous
pieces. The Goldschmidts had their own orchestra, conducted
by Julius Benedict, and their company included some famous
musicians of the day, among them W. H. Weiss, well known as
an opera and oratorio singer; H. W. Ernst, who was a virtuoso
on the violin; Piatti, the celebrated Italian cellist and friend
of Joachim; and Lablache, the son of Jenny's former singing
companion. At the beginning of the tour she wrote to Amalia:

LVI

Brighton, December 20, 1855

Amalia, dear heart:

It has grieved us very much to learn of your misfortune. We
had not the slightest notion of it. Poor Rudolph, and poor you!
How in the world did you go through it all? As always, you
don't say a single word about your own feelings. Oh, my dear
Amalia!

We are both so very sorry that you three have had to go
through such difficult months. Only, after all, everything must
have been God's will. I hope that you are all well again now
and that you will be able to celebrate the great Christmas Feast
together.

Protect little Rudolph from the terrible —————.[44]

We are very well, thank the Lord. Walter is splendid. He gets

[44] This almost illegible word is, we believe, *Breune,* a phonetic mis-
spelling for *Bräune,* which means quinsy or croup.

bigger every day and is saying everything now. *Vevey* did the child a lot of good.

We have decided to spend the winter in England so as to give concerts there. I am feeling fine. My voice is very good. Otto is in excellent health too, praise God. We have already given three concerts in London; I did *The Creation* and *Elijah* in London, and everything went off just as we wished it. We are now thinking about earning money, and then adieu, my public! This is our last musical tour. We have rented a nice house three-quarters of an hour from London where Walter can have good air. Naturally, Josephine stays with Walter when I make little trips into London, and in this way I am free from worry about the child. It wasn't easy to give up our house in Dresden for the winter, and it is costing us a bit of a struggle to come once more into such close contact with the world. Except that the results are so splendid that it is really worth the trouble to put oneself out a little!

I was aghast at the death of Frau Lenné.[45] That fine man! If you see him please tell him how deeply I regret his terrible loss and how I sympathize with him. So *their* house, too, is virtually locked up. Oh, life is stern and terrible. If only we would observe our true relationship to God and to eternity with befitting earnestness!

Perhaps we shall be together next Christmas, Amalia of my heart! Meanwhile, adieu! Both of us send our sincerest greetings to all of you. May God bless you. Please greet Taubert when you see him, that good person. So, once more farewell. May heaven watch over you all.

Your loving and thankful
Jenny G.

(P.S.) My address until the spring is Laurel House, High Street, Putney, London.

In March the tour was interrupted for a concert in aid of the Nightingale Fund. Sidney Herbert, who was a mutual friend of Florence Nightingale and Jenny, had introduced the two ladies. Jenny, ever mindful of charity and of a good cause, became interested in the idea of raising money for the improve

---

[45] Wife of the well-known landscape gardener.

ment of nursing. The concert took place in Exeter Hall on March 11, and raised £1,872 for the fund. The Goldschmidts paid all expenses, and Julius Benedict and Lablache waived their fees. Our collection includes the programme belonging to Sidney Herbert himself and with his notations on the cover.

Later in the spring there was a concert at Buckingham Palace, and a command performance, the first in England, of Schumann's *Paradise and Peri*. This took place at the Philharmonic Society's rooms in Hanover Square on June 23, the conductor being Sterndale Bennett. Queen Victoria and Prince Albert were there, besides King Oscar II of Sweden, and Mme. Schumann, spending her first season in England, was also present. Although Jenny often sang the airs from *Paradise and Peri*— for she was an admirer as well as a friend of Schumann—it never reached the height of popular acclaim, though Clara Schumann wrote of her interpretation that she was "the most magnificent Peri imaginable".

After such a long and taxing season, Jenny was exhausted. She went to Kissingen for a rest and to take a cure, and afterwards visited Norderney for the sea-bathing. She returned to Dresden for the winter via Hamburg and Berlin. Our collection contains a letter written during this period :

LVII
Norderney, September 22, 1856

My dear Amalia :

Thank heaven, I can gather from your lines of September that things are going better for you and father as well as for Rudolph and his family. I was so glad to hear again from all of you.

We are getting along fine too. We are here simply to enjoy the air and the bathing. But it will soon be so cold that we shall have to leave. I am very glad that it suits just as well for us to go to Berlin about the 20th of October, and if we have to stay a few days there before you come, it won't matter. Don't let yourself be persuaded, therefore, to leave Rudolph sooner than you had originally planned, for, as I have said, the time schedule will come out just right : on the 3rd or 4th we shall arrive in Hamburg; we shall stay there fourteen days, and then go on to Berlin.

I have no objections to what you plan to do about copying my portrait, except that I should not like to find myself in Count R's house even as a picture. And it seems that they begin sketching the same face two or three times without consulting the original picture on your wall. Thus, these copies lose all their value. And Countess Schönborn has it in Vienna, of course. But more about this when we see one another again.

I am overjoyed at the idea of pressing you and father to my heart again, and once more I greet Rudolph, his wife and their little treasure, and commend all of you into God's protection— I kiss you, dear Amalia, as I do father, and remain steadfastly

Your
Jenny G.

Back in Dresden once more, Jenny sent the following letter :

LVIII

Dresden, October 30, 1856

Dear Amalia :

We arrived happy and in good health. On Monday I went immediately for the black material like my coat, and you can still get some exactly like it. You can have six ells of it, and that is quite enough. It is two ells wide. However, you can obtain more of it, if necessary. It costs about four Thaler per ell. Will you be good enough to let me know soon whether you would like to have any of it?

We hope to hear soon that you have decided to come here for Christmas. We are looking forward to it very much. Our house has a charming view. I am very healthy and strong and *know* already that I am carrying my second child.

May God bless you. My best greetings to father, from

Your loving,
Jenny G.

P.S. As for the letter from "Sweden", Goldschmidt will clarify it himself.

A note followed shortly afterward:

LIX
Dresden, November 8, 1856

Dear Amalia:

I wrote to you about eleven or twelve days ago to tell you that you can have some of that coat material. Will you be good enough to let me know whether or not you want to have it? I mean by return mail. Otherwise the merchant cannot hold it any longer. Also, tell me how many ells you need. It comes very wide, about two ells, and costs approximately four Thalers. Did you fail to receive my letter about it?

Yours,

Jenny G.

On March 31, 1857, the Goldschmidts had their second child, Jenny. The widow of the Bishop of Norwich, Mrs. Stanley, became godmother to this baby.

The Goldschmidts were by now spending so much time in England, and had so many friends there, that they decided to make this country their permanent home. They settled first in Roehampton, at that time a village surrounded by meadows and common land, in a rented house.

A long letter was sent to Mme. Wichmann in December of 1858:

LX
Roehampton Lodge, Roehampton, Surrey, England,
December 15, 1858

My dear Amalia:

Here I am finally sitting down to write a word to you. I received your last letter promptly, and if I didn't live so much partly *in the clouds* and partly in this never ceasing activity since October, you would have heard from me long ago. Before you wrote the first time about Otto's daguerreotype, I had already packed it up with some other things.

For a long time we have been looking for a *permanent* house here, but we have only just found one. Therefore I could not get at the trunks in which the daguerreotypes were put, for we had to store all our things in the local pantechnicon because of lack of space. I hope to have these treasures back in my hands in two or three weeks, and will send them to you as soon as an opportunity presents itself. Unless perhaps you wish to have them at once, even though the postage cost would come rather high.

I am delighted to hear that Rudolph and his family are now staying with you, and that little Rudolph is cheering up Gross-Papa and Gross-Mama. One thing is sure : I understand how you feel, and that you will never be free of your pain. But something sublime lies hidden in a real sorrow, and such a sorrow teaches us to look at this earthly life more in the proper perspective, just as there is certainly nothing in the world more important for us than that we should direct our desires *heaven-ward*.

We are all very well, thank heaven, and like being in England. The children are blooming and we are situated in a very plea-sant neighbourhood here. But the fog at this time of year is really terrible. An hour ago (ten o'clock in the morning) it was com-pletely dark, so that we had to light the lights. Otherwise, though, the whole summer up to the end of October was indescribably beautiful.

Dear Amalia, would you like to do me a great favour ! When you go driving, please go by Gerson's. He has sent me a small bill for a coat which I bought there a year and a half ago (for 15 Thaler), and I simply can't imagine how I could have for-gotten to pay it. Therefore, may I ask you to tell him that I have not sent the money yet because I want to look among all my bills to see if his is among them, and I can't do so until the trunk which contains your daguerreotypes becomes accessible to me. For this reason I should like to ask him to wait for a while yet. Will you do this for me?

May Christmas time bring peace and quiet joy to all of you. My thoughts will be with you just as if you were my real parents.

Those wonderful days with all of you in Berlin will never come back again. Greetings to my dear father, also to Rudolph and to Herr Herrmann, and may the Lord take you all under his protection.

Your true, devoted

Jenny Goldschmidt

Amalia's husband, the noted sculptor, died shortly before the following letter was sent to Amalia. If the tone of this letter seems strange and exaggerated, there were reasons for it. Jenny was shocked to hear of the death of Professor Wichmann, whom she considered to be her foster-father, and she felt a deep concern for her beloved, widowed friend. Moreover, the letter from Amalia to which she is replying here may have contained despondent statements which Jenny sought to refute by her fervid religious affirmations. Jenny's phraseology, which might have sounded grandiloquent from any other pen than hers, is quite sincere and arose from her innate religious feeling.

LXI

Eastbourne, July 28, 1859

My dear Amalia:

To think that you could write to me in this time of trouble and not say a word in it about yourself and your health! Now, my good Amalia! I have so often seen how, in this life, the happiness of a family can vanish in one or two years. My dear friend, you have gone through very difficult times. It pains me that I could not be with you during all these troubles. If I had been free, you would have had a daughter at your side and my old true friend and father would have had a loving hand to care for him. You know, my beloved Amalia, how it is when one has children in the house!

Look to heaven, and then in this transient world you will never seek salvation or *healing* except through the *Great Healer!* Look for Him, seek Him, dear sister. Oh, if I had not found Him, how worldly and vain I should probably be now from so much admiration! But the image of the Cross has made me humble! Dear soul, do likewise. I love you so much. You have always been so good and kind to me that I should like with all my heart to offer you something worthy in return. Oh, what could be more splendid than that I should lead my Amalia directly up the road to Golgotha, there alone to seek consolation in her sorrow and peace for her soul? There is only one name through which we can become blessed, and this name is *Jesus Christ*, and His blood cleanses us from our many sins—and sins we all have aplenty.

Please don't neglect what I am saying, dear Amalia. You yourself gave my little Walter a Bible. In it is written everything that I should like to say to you now. I should not love you if I did not open my heart to you at a time when God alone—and not human beings—can and will console one. May the peace of God which passeth all understanding be over you and yours.

I am not going to take back the photo of Otto.[46] You must not try to make me. You must keep it as long as you live, and if you should die before I do I will get it back again. I don't want a copy of it either. Nothing can replace the original for me. But if you should send it (the original) back to me then you'll get it right back again—after all, it is really in its right place with you.

I thank you most sincerely for the gift of ———'s cup.[47] I shan't see either until I go home in about three weeks, and then I will write you my thanks once more. Meanwhile, please do not write me any answer to these lines and don't misunderstand them. They contain the holiest things, and it would give me infinite pleasure to know that you share them with me. Read your Bible. Consolation and the promise of blessedness lies in it for those who hear God's word and heed it. And so may God lead you to the light.

In faithful love,
Your devoted
Jenny Goldschmidt

(P.S.) What a dear person Herrmann is, and how mature he has become!

[46] It is difficult to establish the identity of the "Otto" in the photograph. Apparently, it was her husband rather than Amalia Wichmann's son.

[47] The word for cup, *Tasse*, is clear in Jennys handwriting, but the preceding word is illegible.

The next letter was written from their second home in England, overlooking Wimbledon Common. As it indicates, a big tour in Ireland was being planned. Joachim and Belletti accompanied them in this venture. In Dublin Jenny sang in the *Messiah,* and it is of interest to note that Sir Charles Stanford,[48] then aged seven, was very much impressed at her singing of the words, "And they were sore afraid", in a whisper which reached to every corner of the hall.

LXII

Argyle Lodge, Wimbledon Common, September 6, 1859
My dear Amalia:
I found your beautiful presents when I got back from Solbad, and I thank you from the bottom of my heart for thinking of me with so much love. I had no idea that you intended to give me the beautiful cup with Herrmann's song[49] on it, and I was most pleasantly surprised when I unpacked it. I must thank you most warmly for the drawing of Otto.

I am sorry that you returned the daguerreotype. I am beside myself that Herrmann took my joke seriously when I remarked that it was especially regretful to give away the original! I shall not rest until you have it again. It is in the proper hands with you as the Mother.

I am deeply thankful that you are feeling somewhat stronger. Good, kind Herrmann will certainly brighten your life with his generous, lovable nature. It seems to me quite right that you are alone with him now. Whatever my Amalia does, she will cer-

---

[48] Sir Charles Villiers Stanford, the Irish composer. His instrumental works include six symphonies, many chamber compositions, songs, madrigals, etc.

[49] This could be a reference to the traditional Teutonic hero, Hermann (Arminius), the leader of the Germanic tribes, who defeated the Romans under Varus in the year 9 A.D. A number of patriotic songs and one drama by Kleist, "Die Hermannsschlacht", have been written about this national hero. On the other hand, the Herrmann referred to may be Herrmann Wichmann, and the "song" could refer either to a lyric composed by him or to his favourite lyric.

tainly let me know. It naturally lies close to my heart to know how things go with you.

I am very healthy and strong again. So are my children. They are still by the sea, but they will be back in a week or eight days.

Josephine (my servant) is with Thérèse. Her sister is now here with me as cook, and I am managing, but she finds nothing suitable for her.[50] It is a blessing for me to escape from English food.

We are going to Ireland for several weeks in order to give a number of concerts there. This will be my very last concert trip. And we would not have made this one if the house in which we now live had not been so expensive to furnish. Furniture is excessively (or as they say in English—*horribly*) expensive.

That you, my dear Amalia, believe in God, I do not doubt in the least. That faith is held by most people. What I meant to convey was our justification in Christ, who has paid God the debt of our sins. We weak human beings cannot keep His law even in the best and most active of lives. Therefore, we should offend against His natural laws if we did not take Christ as our Mother, considering ourselves to be saved not through our own deeds but through the Blood of Christ which was poured out for us. We should consider our deeds, our loftiest deeds, that is, as the result simply of our belief in Christ, and not at all as if we could buy salvation for ourselves through such acts of ours. This is the point of contention, dear Amalia, against which I should like to make objection. For we are all inclined to make ourselves worthy through our good works or in the fulfilling of our duty. But such self-justification is not acceptable to God, who is himself the embodiment of perfection. *This is what I meant,* dear Amalia, and may the Lord help us to achieve this knowledge of our imperfections. We should not look to our own insufficient works but rather to the merits of Christ—eternally acceptable to God.

My husband sends you his warmest regards, and we both hope that you and Herrmann will come to England soon. By the way, he has left his white scarf [tie][51] here.

[50] Reference being, no doubt, to her dislike of local fare.
[51] "Halsbindel" is the German word here.

May God Almighty be with you and yours is the prayer of your
Jenny G.

During the year 1860 things were fairly quiet for the Gold-schmidts, since Jenny was preparing to give birth to their third and last child, Ernst Svend David Goldschmidt, born in January, 1861. Towards the end of the year 1860 we find these comments in a letter to Amalia:

LXIII
Argyle Lodge, Parkside, Wimbledon Common, London, S W
December 4, 1860

Dear Amalia:

My most heartfelt thanks for your recent affectionate lines. I have been on my feet for the last four or five weeks, and in the circumstances I am getting along very well. This letter, there-fore, is not a notice of the arrival of Number 3! But this time it deals with a matter which is completely new to me and one which I beg you very much not to get angry about.

A friend of mine here has begged me to give her a letter of recommendation to you for an Englishwoman who is coming to Berlin. She asks no more than perhaps to pay one visit. I pro-mised *nothing* because I told her that probably you would not be able to receive anybody. She is a Miss Dixon, who is going to Berlin to paint Princess Victoria for Queen Victoria. She is being sent by the Queen to paint the children as well as the Princess. Miss Dixon is said to be very talented and likeable. Whether she is, I just don't know. She is coming simply with my visiting card. If you can see her, it will be very kind of you. If not, then I have prepared her for that eventuality too. Are you very angry with me?

We are all well. I am longing for my release.

I plan soon to write to Herrmann. May God be with you.
Your
Jenny Goldschmidt

LXIV

Argyle Lodge, Parkside, Wimbledon Common, London, SW

April 30, 1861

My dear Amalia:

I am back at my writing desk at last, and can send you a few lines that I have owed you for such a long time. I have my hands full with work of all kinds. And in England one is hardly able to keep up with the daily "notes" which are sent to one from all sides.

How are you now, my Amalia? Were you perhaps unwell again this winter? I am so sorry that Herrmann is suffering so much with his head. He should find a nice wife for himself, and that would probably be the best thing for him, though I am the last person who would push anybody into marriage. Meanwhile, many natures must do it, perhaps.

I am getting along better, but I am very worn out with the additional work with my third child. Besides, I do not believe that the English climate will ever agree with me.

I have not written to you since my delivery. I truly don't have to, because I have you so often in my thoughts. I lost my milk after the sixth week because I had a severe attack of colic and got costive. As a result of this terrible stuffing which the doctors recommend for their patients here, I was very miserable and thus the little rascal had to be brought up on a bottle, and so far that is going quite superbly, thank the Lord. He is a healthy, strong child, and already very fetching. He seems to have just the same disposition as the two others. So I shall not be idle. Meanwhile, I have come to love the little fellow very much. He will be called *Ernst*. He was baptized on the 17th of March in the Church.

Walter is making progress at school, but in the autumn he will have a tutor at home. I should like so very much to see little Rudolph. Does he look like his Papa?

My Amalia, can you please let me know your plans for the summer? I shall probably have to do something for myself, and I have a plan for next winter that I hope very much to carry out. But I won't say any more about it, since I have not even mentioned it to my husband yet. But couldn't we make plans so that we could all be together somewhere this summer or autumn? That would be a great joy for me. Now, if you have already made your own arrangements, be sweet and let me know at your convenience.

Professor Magnus has sent me a copy of my picture. He has succeeded extremely well. I cannot deny that it gave me great pleasure to possess a copy of that particular picture for my children. I am the artist who worked for them (the children) and who achieved their independence. And then, that was the only happy, carefree period of my life—when I lived with all of you in the Hasenheger. Many things were different for you, too! Yes, this life is only a temporary dwelling. But our home is in the beyond, and it must be reached through the mediation of Christ. May we all leave this world one day trusting in his *wounds* and not through any merits of our own. For how far we always are from what we ought to be and could be, and what would become of us if we did not have a defender and intermediary!

Goldschmidt is well, but he needs a change of air. We have all suffered more or less from throat infections and rheumatism. Only the children have been quite healthy the whole time, except for an attack of coughing in March (a bad month in England).

My husband sends his very best greetings. What is Taubert doing? Are he and his wife still having children? Or hasn't the *possibility* ceased yet?

Greetings to Rudolph and Herrmann from
Your devotely loving
Jenny Goldschmidt
(P.S.) Do you ever see anything of the Music-Count??

After Ernst was born the Goldschmidts bought a piece of land in Wimbledon Park, where, before her marriage, Jenny Lind used to ride with the Duke of Wellington. Here they built, among the rhododendrons, a comfortable house with many tall Tudor chimneys and a good deal of living space. In the distance they could view the Crystal Palace and marvel at the fireworks at night. They moved to their new home in 1864, and here they were visited by many friends and musicians. Among them was Arthur Sullivan, the first Mendelssohn Scholar, not yet famous, while many guests from abroad found a path to the Goldschmidts. Mme. Albani stopped at Oak Lea with one of her first introductions.

Though Jenny was hospitable and warm with her friends, and with strangers who observed the proper decorum, she could still be cool or even haughty towards those who she felt were forcing themselves upon her as curious intruders or celebrity seekers. This trait became more pronounced as she grew older, calling for much tact and unobtrusive intervention by Otto. Once, when two young men appeared by surprise while Jenny was reposing in her garden, she bristled at the reason for their intrusion, which was simply that they were curious to see what the "Swedish Nightingale" was like. Drawing herself up to her full height, she bowed, and said : "This is what my front is like, and"—turning around completely—"this is what my back is like. Now you know!" And with that she made a hasty retreat.

This anecdote, of course, could be apocryphal, but, true or not, it captures Jenny's general attitude to the idly curious public that was constantly encroaching upon her privacy.

She always retained a fondness for Swedish customs and her native cuisine, and there were always Swedes among the employees in the household. Thus the children were well cared for when their parents travelled in Europe to give concerts. Mlle. Josephina Ahmansson stayed with the Goldschmidts after their marriage and became their housekeeper. To the children she was "auntie". She outlived Jenny Lind by some years.

In July, 1861, the Goldschmidts embarked on a series of concerts, one of them held "by the obliging permission of the Earl of Dudley" at Dudley House as a benefit performance for the Society of Female Artists. A performance of *Elijah* was given at Exeter Hall in aid of the church and school work at the Victoria Docks. This was followed by twenty-four concerts in the North of England and Scotland. Most of these were made up of miscellaneous items, but in Edinburgh the *Creation* was sung, and in Bradford the *Messiah*. Otto Goldschmidt conducted the orchestra, accompanied Jenny and played pianoforte solos. Once again Belletti and Piatti were among those who made up their party.

The following letter touches upon the life of that time :

LXV

Eastbourne, Sussex, England, September 10, 1861

Beloved Amalia :

It seems as if I'm not really happy about your friendly gift, the three daguerreotypes sent with your last letters. But they gave me great pleasure. Herrmann's and Rudolph's are beautifully successful. And little Rudolph looks so good. What a blessing Rudolph has this child. Better one than ten! Although I shouldn't like to lose a single one of my three. We should like so much to send you one of *Baby,* but so far he has been too young. Now we have made a half-hearted attempt, and it has turned out quite similar to the others. You must not notice my embarrassed face. He can't sit up, and we didn't want to have him photographed with his nurse. Otto's picture is for Herrmann, and the others are for you.

Well, what is poor Herrmann doing now? How sorry we are that he is in such pain. The grape-cure in Merano did me a lot of good, and also Bad Kissingen and sea baths. I never have headaches now, or at least very seldom, and I was a martyr to them. There must be a remedy if the doctors find out the source of the pain. I believe England would be good for Herrmann.

And how are you feeling, dear Amalia? Perhaps you will send me a few lines some time before Christmas, to bring me up-to-date in your doings and actions.

I have felt very weak after the work with Ernest,[52] since I still have to spend a large part of my time looking after my first son, and then the staircases in these English houses are killing me. Otherwise, I believe that I have become stronger, healthier, and more cheerful. My voice is better than it was several years ago, and so this autumn I intend to make a "little tour" in England.

Otto has bought a small piece of land in the neighbourhood where we are now living, and we plan to build a little house on it. And to this purpose I will stretch my wings once more. I sang at a concert in London on the fourth of July and it went magnificently.

The children are very healthy and strong. They are growing very much in length and breadth. Walter has a teacher now

[52] Jenny is using the English spelling for her third child.

Facsimile of letter to Thackeray's daughter, enclosing tinted
print of the writer

1. In Verdi's opera, "I Masnadieri."   3. Jenny Lind at Exeter Hall.   5. Maria, in "La Figlia del Reggimento."
2. "Lucia di Lammermoor."   4. Alice, in "Roberto il Diavolo."   6. Suzanna, in "Le Nozze di Figaro."

"Jenny Lind in some of her most celebrated characters"
(*Illustrated London News* of November 12th 1887, ten days
after her death)

who comes every day from nine to two. And a little *child* is taking lessons with him. So I hope that we are taken care of for the next two years. As far as his studies are concerned, he likes to work and has a great facility in everything. Jenny is very sly, comical, deep and warm, but like granite. She has an interesting character when she is understood and is handled with a great deal of love. I have a charming girl looking after her. Jenny is very musical and, like Walter, she has a powerful voice. Baby is a most lovable child, so quiet and healthy. He didn't sleep during the first seven months and was very restless. But now he is the best child to take care of and is everybody's treasure, from the kitchen maid up to his Papa and Mama. Ernest is now eight months old. He has four teeth and is thriving splendidly on cow and donkey milk. After six weeks I could not nurse him, and soon after that we bought a female ass, and it helped us no end so that the child never takes medicine (a thing that I hate so and fear so much for little children !).

It is very beautiful where we are.[53] The ocean lies in front of us with the most beautiful wheatfields reaching down to the water—and marvellous air. I just wish that Herrmann would come to visit us at Christmas. Here with us he could be completely quiet. With God's help, at the beginning of December we shall be back home, since we shall only be away for four or five weeks. If only our good Herrmann would do this?

What is Taubert doing? Give him my greetings if you see him once more among the living. I long to see my friends in Germany. I hope, God willing, that this will surely take place next summer.

Josephine is with us. I believe she would die if she had to leave us. And yet she is so awkward and difficult to handle that we often wish she had stayed in Sweden with her family, with a good pension from us. Meanwhile, we are very grateful to her, of course. She is true and dependable as few are !

May God be with you and yours. In love, your devoted

Jenny Goldschmidt

P.S. Our address is still Wimbledon Common.

In January, 1862, the tour of which Jenny spoke took place,

[53] Conjectured from the context, one word being illegible.

and concerts were given in fifteen towns. Once again the pro-
grammes were miscellaneous, but the tour ended with a performance of the *Creation* at Norwich and the *Messiah* at Northampton. In addition Jenny and her husband gave three oratorios
in London during the International Exhibition in 1862.

A year later, in March 1863, Jenny was invited to sing at the
wedding of the Prince of Wales and Princess Alexandra of
Denmark. The chorale which she sang had been composed by
the Prince Consort.

A highlight of this year was Otto Goldschmidt's revival of
Handel's *Allegro* and *Il Penseroso,* in which Jenny Goldschmidt
of course took part. In June she was one of the performers at a
matinée presented by M. and Mme. Lablache in the Queen's
Concert Rooms, Hanover Square. She sang a Rossini duet with
Lablache, a Swedish melody, and Haydn's canzonetta, "My
mother bids me bind my hair", which she had recently added to
her repertoire, and which became so closely associated with her
name. She also went to Germany to take part in the Düsseldorf
Musical Festival. Otto was engaged to conduct, which he did so
well that he surpassed even Jenny's expectations.

The following letter to Amalia gives insight into the life of
the Goldschmidts in the mid-1860's :

LXVI
                    Oak Lea, Wimbledon Park, May 6, 1864
My beloved Amalia :

I am very much touched by your last letter, and this time at
least you will not have to wait long for an answer.

I want to thank you most warmly for your *faithfulness,* and
to assure you absolutely that I am not an ungrateful recipient
of such expressions of love. My heart really became more aglow
than usual when I read your last letter, and with every word
beautiful, ancient, irretrievable times appeared so clearly before
my eyes and my soul that it seemed as if I were young once
more and were living only for my exalted art, without cares and
without any preoccupation !

Oh ! Things are different once life becomes serious and its

cares begin to oppress one as if they wanted to pull one down into the depths. Alas, everything changes when youth has fled.

For the first time I have been happy enough to learn, my dear Amalia, that *you* are really a little better, and this slight improvement (unfortunately slight) makes me deeply happy and thankful because now I can hope that from now on you will enjoy better health, and may God show you his mercy in this way.

I regret very much to hear of Herrmann's illness. Can't he perhaps go somewhere where he might find relief for his nerves? Isn't there a place in Italy which could bring him back to health? But that's the way life is; we all have to go through suffering and fire. If only all this happens for the good of our souls, then we shall not have suffered in vain. I am very sorry that you are also worried about Rudolph. May God grant recovery to you all.

Last Sunday I saw the aged Buttner. Actually I was going from Düsseldorf to Wiesbaden for three weeks (because of a neuralgic condition in my shoulder which I fortunately got rid of). The old man is still very lively, but he is afraid of leaving his accustomed *nest,* and he went back to Frankfurt immediately. He always talks of Rudolph with much affection.

Düsseldorf will very likely be my last excursion, as I fear I cannot sing any more because my old throat has become so dry. I now sing only a very little, for myself and my friends. It is a shame to have to grow old just at *the moment* when constant practice, experience and deep feeling combine so fittingly with art and religion and make one's performance into a *spiritual* experience. But resignation is the key word to life, and blessed be the name of the Lord!

Through God's grace, we are all very well. I have never been so well in my whole life as I have been here for about the last two years. The air where we are living is most invigorating. If Herrmann came here to our house for the winter and remained until the spring—just where we are living—I believe he would recover remarkably well. I left all my severe headaches at Wimbledon Common. He would be really welcome, I can assure you.

Yes, we have been in our new house for about two months. We built it ourselves and we cannot be thankful enough that we were permitted to have a house like this in such surroundings. We are delighted, and, although everything has just been newly planted, nevertheless growing things bloom and flourish so profusely here that we hope to become covered in *green* in a few years. I mean, to see the house overgrown with creeping vines. For on our property we already have some very beautiful old trees. The children feel like birds, and the children and the birds sing to one another all day long!

Walter works very hard, and in the autumn he is going to a preparatory school just near us which has an excellent reputation. I shall have the pleasure of having him home every second Saturday until Monday, and English boys have plenty of holidays: five weeks at Christmas, two weeks at Easter, and in summer seven weeks vacation. That makes fourteen weeks out of the year, and so we can keep our close contact with each other. Walter likes to study and indeed is a good child, but other boys will be good for him and will, I hope, help him to get rid of his irritability.

Jenny is very like me, I believe, and not the easiest child to handle. She needs much love but is yet very *warm* and *deep,* and is affectionate with me.[54] I still have no governess for her, and I am instructing her myself, but in addition she has a delightful English nurse who has been with us for many years.

Little Ernst is lively, very healthy and strong, like the other two. A sweet boy, I believe he has the best *character* of the three. My husband is very well—always in good health, thank the Lord—and he has undertaken to instruct several pupils (in piano) at the *Royal Academy,* and that takes him to London every Saturday and Wednesday. We also have some pleasant friends here now, and living is fine in England, if only it were not so expensive.

[54] Jenny Lind's appraisal of her daughter was loving and clear-sighted. It is echoed, more than a century later, by her great-granddaughter, Mrs. Oliver Woods. She says of her grandmother, of whom she was very fond, "She was forceful and temperamental, loyal and generous—and she *could* only be ruled by love. She adored Jenny Lind, and she used to play all the Swedish and German music to me when we were alone. Music seemed to spring from her as a gift from God—*not* manufactured. They must have been alike. They had fierce tempers and loving hearts."

Marie Mendelssohn[55] has been living near us for a short time, and I am very happy about this. She is at home alone all day long because her husband is in London; she has no children, and a *clod of a husband he is,* between you and me. It is very strange to me to have Mendelssohn's daughter here. Il mondo è rotondo![56]

The English have really played *havoc* with Garibaldi, and many persons, including myself, would be *very happy* if the good man would go back to Caquera.

My husband would like to go somewhere in Switzerland this summer. Perhaps we can meet somewhere there. And now, dear Amalia, I must close with many cordial greetings to all who still remember me—(Meyerbeer has now also gone to his fore-fathers)[57]—i.e., to Professor Werder, Taubert, Dir. Lenné, the Privy Councilor Jüngken,[58] good old lady Schröder(n), etc., etc. May the good Lord be with them all, my old friends. My heart still beats for all of them, but mostly for you and yours, my faithful Amalia.

God bless you, says your loving
Jenny Goldschmidt

The Goldschmidts' house was always full of music. Arthur Sullivan continued to be a frequent visitor, and Coleridge sang duets with her, which he found an anxious business. Otto Goldschmidt had accepted the post of Vice-Principal of the Royal Academy of Music. Sterndale Bennett was then Principal, and the two of them were working together in the publication and translation of German chorales. In connection with this work Otto made several journeys to Leipzig and elsewhere. He had also been appointed honorary organist at the church at West Hill, about a mile from Oak Lea. He was playing much Beethoven, Bach and Chopin at this time, and accompanied his wife

[55] Mrs. Victor Benecke.
[56] Literally, "The world is round." Probably Jenny meant to signify something like, "How small the world is!" or some similar expression of pleased astonishment at meeting old friends in unexpected places.
[57] Meyerbeer died on May 2, 1863.
[58] Professor Jüngken was a famous physician who had been attached to the Court of Berlin.

in Schubert, Schumann and Mendelssohn, especially the latter's *Schilflied, Nachtlied* and *Auf Flügeln des Gesanges,* and
Schumann's *Dichter Liebe* and *Stille Tränen.* Though Jenny
only performed in public on special occasions, she often sang at
home for her family and friends, and at bedtime for the children
she would end up with Schumann's *Wenn fromme Kindlein
schlafen gehen.*

They went to Sweden several times, and on one occasion took
the children with them. They were always welcomed by the
Royal Family. And they had, of course, to look after Jenny's
financial affairs there, and the charities which were so close to
her heart.

LXVII

Brighton, November 15, 1864

My Beloved Amalia :

It gave me very great pleasure to have news once more of you
and yours, and I am very grateful to Herrmann for writing me
such a lovable letter. Unfortunately, however, it seems that I
never receive anything but sad news from you all—and now I
learn that you have been so sick again, my dear Amalia ! It often
makes me feel very bitter to live so far from my old friends and
acquaintances, so that I never have the consolation of your company and that of your family. But we have arranged things in
this way for the greater well-being of our children, and so we
must put up with the unfortunate aspect of this arrangement.
The older one becomes, however, the more deeply one recalls
the impressions of youth, and certainly one loves more deeply and
warmly those whom one loved in youth. At least, that's how I
feel about you, dear Amalia—and how affectionate you have
always been toward me ! And how can I ever thank you for still
loving your old Jenny so faithfully, even now ?

But do tell me what is wrong with you. I feel so close to you
that I should really know everything that concerns you. May the
mild air in Pau give you strength and improved health, and, if
it is written thus in God's palm, may your life be prolonged

for many years yet for the sake of your two sons, whose happiness you embody in so many ways!

I consider it to be an act of God's grace that good Herrmann is at present somewhat restored to health, so that he can stand by you and give you the help which his tender, loving heart renders with such full measure of joy. Oh, if he could only get rid of his headaches!

Bad Kissingen, then England, and the (passing) years have cured me. If only you two would plan to come to see us in the spring! Even though it is not big, our house is nice and comfortable and located in the most beautiful, healthy place, and I somehow have the feeling that the English air would be of the utmost benefit to both of you! Just think, Amalia, if you would consent to pay us a long visit in the spring, what a great, great joy it would be to me to be able to pay back to you and Herrmann even in this smallest measure all that you so often and so magnanimously did for me! And how happy Otto would be to welcome you here. Do think about it, my beloved Amalia. Do not refuse my warm invitation but come once in your lifetime to see old England and old Jenny!!

Praise and thanks be to the Lord that we are all well! The children are prospering, and my Walter has been at school since the beginning of September. I only see him every second Sunday till Monday morning; at least on those Sundays I can have him with me in Church. He is at a good school—we have every reason to believe so—run by a Dr. Huntingford in Wimbledon, half-an-hour's walk from our house. The young fellow had so few playmates that our only solution was to send him away from here. He longed so much for the friendship of other boys, and yet at the same time he is so shy and so excitable when he sees other boys, that we hope it will do him good to be rather severely knocked about as they do in these English schools. But there is so much healthy, powerful play in the air that the boys simply cannot help being inured to hardship by it. Up to now he has been getting along fine. He was transferred to a fairly advanced class right at the beginning, so at least he doesn't have to go through the lowest classes. It is still difficult for him to go back to school after he has been at home, but he is bearing up well and is quite fearful of appearing *weak* to the other young

boys. In English schools there are almost four months' vacation
every year, so that the students' contact with their parents is not
lost.

Jenny is my very favourite companion. We have become extremely close to each other, and I pray to God that I shall not
love her too much. You simply cannot imagine, my dear Amalia,
what a daughter means to a mother's heart. She is worth more
than ten sons (maybe, of course, not ten like your good Herrmann, I grant you that!). She is musical, and has something
very lovable about her. I am enclosing a photograph of her
which was taken recently. As soon as I have one of Walter and
Ernst you shall have them. It is perhaps very selfish of me to
think the pictures could interest you. Only I believe that you
have a tender feeling for my children, and I am sure you understand my wish that you should possess their pictures.

In the New Year I am getting an excellent governess for
Jenny. Up to now, I have instructed her myself, but my knowledge does not stretch very far and, besides, it takes so much out
of me. Mlle. Girard was born in Neuchâtel and has been in
England many years. She speaks several languages, she is
thoroughly and genuinely educated, and I hope she will also
prove to be a companion for me, since otherwise I am very much
alone and seldom have anybody whom I can talk to. She worked
eight years with a much-liked family[59] whom I know, where she
was greatly honoured and loved. May God give his blessing to
this new move!

Ernest is such a lovable child—very musical, and he seems to
be the most talented of the three. He will be four this January.
Jenny will be eight in March, and Walter was eleven in August.
How time flies!

I am stronger than I have even been, although I am approaching an important point of my life. Up to now I have
managed things quite well, and I can't be grateful enough if
they keep on going as they do now. Actually, I sing very seldom
nowadays because for about a year I have felt an uncomfortable

[59] Jenny Maude, in her reminiscences of family life, mentions that Mlle.
Girard had tutored the two sisters of John Addington Symonds. Thus the
reference here is in all probability to the Symonds family.

dryness in my throat. But after drinking ass's milk for three months, I am *so much* better that I was able to sing at a party which we gave.

Otto is well and strong; always the same tender, lovable husband who does not spare any work or effort to make the children and me happy and satisfied. Here in England he enjoys great esteem and trust. My beloved old guardian in Sweden is still lively and energetic and is our truest friend and father. All our dealings in Sweden, which are in his son's hands, are always safely and honestly taken care of. May God grant him many more years of life!

My old Annetta is still alive too. And Josephine is now happier in Sweden. We have nice neighbours and a charming circle of acquaintances here of the best kind : good, true servants (Josephine's sister, my cook, has been with us for many years), and so I can really speak of God's extravagant grace and patience toward me. May His holy name be blessed!

And now, dear Amalia, forgive this long letter. I could not help it. I simply had to write. That God may protect you is the cry of your loving and always thankful—

Jenny Goldschmidt

P.S. Warmest greetings to Herrmann. Otto will write to him soon.

(Along side of first page :) I have been on this south coast of England for several weeks but I am going home at Christmas, God willing. It's beautiful here.

In 1865 Jenny sang in the *Messiah* for the Clergy Fund in London. The following spring she took part in a three-day festival at Hamburg, with her husband conducting.[60] The programme included the *Messiah, St. Cecilia's Ode* and part of the *Paradise and Peri*.

During the same month in which the following letter was written she took part, for the last time, in the Düsseldorf Festival. Afterwards she and her husband paid a visit to the King and Queen of Hanover. Jenny could not sing on this occasion because of a cold, but other artists did perform. This must have been a nerve-racking event, for Hanover was soon to be absorbed

60 Hamburg was Otto Goldschmidt's native city.

into Prussia, and Bismark's army was at the gates. It was with difficulty that the Goldschmidts managed to catch the last train leaving Hanover to rejoin their children at Düsseldorf.

LXVIII

Hanover, June 12, 1866

My dear Amalia :

Please don't be angry with me for keeping you waiting so long for an answer. But we were completely exhausted by our stay in Hamburg, and I could not add letter-writing to my other demanding activities, for then I might not have been able to carry out properly my commitment to the public. Words fail me when I try to tell you how much I should have liked to go to Berlin to see you. But we could not arrange it. We have been terribly in demand, and we are deluged by invitations from all sides in so touching a way that we have already used up much of the limited time at our disposal. And now I have been in Hanover since Thursday. But because of the great demands which were made on me in Hamburg I am totally exhausted— so completely overwrought that I can't speak, I am so hoarse. But I can't wait later than Thursday for this hoarseness to go because we must go home. I have been here exactly a year and haven't seen my Walter since January. So you see, my dear Amalia, we cannot go to Berlin.

I hear again, to my great sorrow, that you and Herrmann are not well, but don't you think that when the first year of the marriage is over he will then have his nerves under control? *How sorry* I am that good old Herrmann cannot enjoy his life with that dear woman. And *you* : I thought that you were much better, my dear, dear Amalia. Life is a never ending struggle, right to the end. Only by suffering do we move toward eternal peace. Everything, you know, is given to us by a loving Father who alone knows what is good for us. "Thy Will Be Done" are the hardest words for our hearts to accept, and yet nothing ever happens that does not stem from love. I can only pray for you very, very fervently. And that I shall do !

I was in Cannes this winter, where it was beautiful beyond

measure. My heart stayed there in the sun, in the flowers, in the olive trees—in the clear atmosphere. Everything here is so poor and colourless. I got my voice back there, too, and was able to take part with my beloved husband in the music festivals both at Düsseldorf and at Hamburg. He has the stuff in him to become a conductor like Mendelssohn. Only he lacks an orchestra that is used to him. All he needs in order to produce the best music is an orchestra conversant with his techniques. I do not love him so much as to be blind; I know I am speaking the truth—and you must put it down to my love and confidence in you that I have spoken so frankly to you about him. For otherwise I should never in any circumstances express my deepest thoughts concerning him to the envious, competitive world. But Otto is gifted far beyond anything I had previously hoped for. He is an angel to me. Oh, indeed, he is like a child to me, dear Amalia. What a blessed feeling it is to be loved by one's husband as I am. Absolute loyalty, inside and out. He is a wonderful person and I grow happier with each year; and after fourteen years that is what one can call *solid* happiness, don't you think?

Our children are magnificent, praise God! As soon as I have good photographs of us all I must send them to you.

Walter has been top of his school ever since Christmas. He is leaving in the summer, probably to go to Rugby, one of the best public schools. He wants to go to *sea,* he says! But Otto will not hear of it. Walter is very lovable and easy to guide. Jenny's character is much like my own. But from her earliest childhood she has been very much sheltered and indulged, and so is already much tenderer and softer. And I have grown terribly attached to her. We feel the same about many things. She has an excellent, exacting governess, and she is learning briskly enough for her age.

Little Ernst is sweet and clever; he will be five years old in January, years which have naturally been spent with me.

Well, I have chatted enough—though I could keep on like this for a long time. God bless you and yours. Thank you for your faithful love. It is truly returned in my deep affection for you.

                              Your loving
                              Jenny Lind Goldschmidt

P.S. How powerful are the impressions of our youth! When I write to you I feel as if I were in your house. I see all the objects there clearly before me!

On July 11 Jenny, now back in London, took part in Arthur Sullivan's Grand Orchestral Concert. She sang "Orpheus and his Lute", which he had dedicated to her, "Sweet Day so Cool", and an air of Handel's.

The following letter was written in a larger hand and appears to be much freer in execution :

LXIX
Dresden, Hotel Belle Vue, November 4 (1866)

Beloved Amalia :

You say once more that you don't know where I am? But, as you see, here we are (we have been here since Saturday). I received both your letters. The first one made me so sad that I didn't know what to think. I got the impression that Herrmann was not happy in his marriage. And then the letter came in which everything seemed to be fine.

We have found so much love and kindness here that it will be difficult to leave it all. Meanwhile, we are planning to go to Berlin on *Monday*. But we are not quite sure whether we can get away then.

No matter how [well] I may find you, Amalia, don't go to any trouble on my behalf. You must not inconvenience yourself for me. If you should be feeling unwell, then I could sit by your bed. After all, I am coming to Berlin for *your sake* alone. You must not let yourself get excited—I am coming. I will leave here on Monday and be at your house on Tuesday at about twelve o'clock, if that is convenient for you. I am telling you this now, so that neither my Amalia nor my good Herrmann need bother about us. Give him the most cordial greetings from both of us, and I greet you, my honoured *mother, sister, friend!*

Auf Wiedersehen! Your

Jenny L. G.

(P.S.) Today is the anniversary of Mendelssohn's death!

By this time Walter was at Rugby. Later he went to Oxford and read Law. Ernst attended Mr. Waterfield's school at East Sheen, and eventually went to Sandhurst and then into the Army. As mentioned in the letters, their sister Jenny was educated at home by her Swiss governess, Mlle. Girard; in later years she became Mrs. Raymond Maude, O.B.E.

As we have seen in the letter of June 12, 1866, Mme. Goldschmidt had begun wintering in the South of France, at Cannes, which Lord Brougham had "discovered" not long before. At that time, however, it was very far from being the fashionable resort which it was later to become.

For her husband's sake, Jenny came once more out of retirement. The Hereford Festival Committee had commissioned him to write an oratorio for their 1867 festival, and he chose the subject of Ruth. He wrote the soprano part, of course, for his wife. She wrote to Judge Munthe that it was solely for Otto's sake that she had the courage to "present her wrinkled old face" to the public, for a wife should be prepared to make any sacrifice for her husband. The reviews were extremely bad. This bitterly angered Jenny, who was always ready to spring to Otto's defence, and two years later she arranged a performance in Hamburg, where it was received with greater enthusiasm. A revival in London, later that year, had a better reception; and two more performances in Düsseldorf followed in 1870 and 1871. On each occasion Jenny sang the soprano part.

LXX

Rose Hotel, Wiesbaden, May 21 (1869)

My dear Amalia:

Your last letter arrived in Hamburg in good time, and now I can thank you for all the love which your words expressed. Unlike most people, you seem to be endowed with the most perfect loyalty, my Amalia! If only the angel child[61] is *really* given the doll, then I shall be quite content. Aunt Jenny commits herself with the greatest of pleasure to deliver a new doll each year if the old one gets broken. Actually, how long does such a child

[61] Herrmann's child.

enjoy a doll? Oh, just a few years. My Jenny had a big one which had an exceptionally beautiful face and which she loved too, and she always had it next to her at breakfast, so that she could surreptitiously put a bit of food into its mouth. For the past two years the doll hasn't accompanied us on our travels, and our governess and I felt a real longing for it. She brought such joy through Jenny's enjoyment. So please give the dear child the doll. Clara will certainly not have anything against it. Please! Please!

It's remarkable how my love for Father and you extends to Herrmann's children. It is very moving how clearly I can see reflected in the younger generation the love I feel for their parents!

Everything went quite beautifully in Hamburg. *Ruth* was really beautifully performed and it enjoyed a most gratifying success. It is very genuine music which one must hear often, for there is nothing in it to titillate the ears, and therefore it cannot be judged immediately by the great mass of listeners. But the criticisms are quite good, and we are happy and thankful. Otto directed it superbly. He had everything so well in command that it flowed out as a perfect whole. Ever since his youth he has been much loved and esteemed there, and everybody was most friendly to us. And the ladies! Why, he always has them in his power, because of his courtesy and tenderness toward them; and since there is a great deal for the women's chorus to sing in *Ruth* the ladies (mostly from good society) were most useful and sang charmingly. I don't believe that another *Ruth* like this one will be heard for a long time, especially so far as the chorus is concerned. Madame Joachim with her beautiful voice sang Naomi quite excellently, and I came through without getting stuck and did my part as well as I could with a throat that was only half well. *March* in *England* was very bad for me, but after earnest supplication to heaven the problem solved itself, and so the Lord came to our aid. For the sake of the friend closest to my heart I wanted to do it if I could.

And now I have the doubtful joy of sitting here alone without my husband or my offspring! Otto accompanied me here, but he left me on Saturday morning to return to our dear children. I have to drink the waters and take baths for my neuralgia. It isn't quite definite yet whether or not Otto will come here with the children. We had all planned to go somewhere in Switzerland, during Walter's vacation, since I should very much like Walter to benefit from the mountain air. When he comes home from school he is always overworked and not properly nourished!! But our plans are not yet quite definite, and therefore I can say nothing for certain.

I should like it very much if we should get together somehow this summer, since you and Clara seem to be alone. I would *love so much* to show you the children, and Jenny would be overjoyed if she could smother Clara's two lovable children with affection, since, like all English children, she is completely *fascinated* by *babies*. Everything will be decided in a few weeks. In any case, I shall stay here long enough for twenty-eight baths, that is until the 21st or 22nd of June. I shall let you know immediately as soon as I have something definite to tell you.

I think it is quite right that Herrmann should go away alone, harsh as that may sound. But in his condition complete rest is the best thing. And Clara also needs rest, for I am afraid that his pain and lack of sleep must be very hard on that *sweet* little woman. Give her my warmest greetings. What news do you have from Herrmann?

If Taubert had shown more energy and *tolerance* in his attitude, then one could not have [illegible word] such a fellow before one's eyes instead of him. I think he (and his wife) can be thankful, although for me his present attitude would be almost a dishonour, for it shows what few traces his activities up to now must have left behind. Perhaps I am wrong, however.[62]

Beloved Amalia!

Your loving,
Jenny L. Goldschmidt

The winters in Cannes, which the Goldschmidts enjoyed so much—not least because of the many friends they met there—were for the time being brought to an end by the Franco-Prussian War. They spent the winter of 1871-72 in Florence, and

[62] It is our conjecture that this enigmatic paragraph refers to problems connected with Taubert's professional career as a composer.

Jenny was able to see the work of the Italian painters in their native land, as she had always wanted to do.

About this time, as she wrote to Judge Munthe, Jenny and her husband were considering a plan to leave England—where, however much she loved the country and its people, the climate was extremely bad for her neuralgia and rheumatism—and live in Germany. The idea was that they would start a musical institute in Wiesbaden, and run it together. The project, however, came to nothing.

LXXI

28 Lung Arno Nuovo, Florence, January 9, 1872

My dear Amalia:

I received your dear lines of the 17th November here in Florence, and I ought to have written in answer to them a long time ago. We have been here since the 17th of October. We first thought of going to Cannes, but we thought that with our German name it would not be advisable to go to France this winter. Also, I was looking for a day school for Jenny and Ernest, and there was nothing of this kind in Cannes. Moreover, we wanted to see something of Italy. Do you know Florence, by any chance? The climate is disagreeable and cannot be compared with that of the Riviera. It is very cold and windy and heavy fogs are very frequent here, too. So I don't feel as well here as at Cannes. Otherwise I can't complain.

Otto, of course, is with me, and the children are continuing to study here. Jenny is going to a deaconess's school directed by nuns from [illegible]. It is very good. I cannot have her taught by a governess any longer. She gets so tired of the same face every day.

Walter is in England, studying for an examination at Oxford, where he will probably be accepted at the University in the Spring. We shall probably stay here until the end of March or April, and then we shall travel back north—perhaps through *Cannes*.

We were in the Bavarian Alps this past summer, where it was quite marvellously beautiful. The boys climbed all over the mountains, and Walter and Ernest are like mountain goats. We were also in Oberammergau to see the Passion Play, which was really very interesting because of the simplicity and the serious-ness with which the local performers played the holy scenes.

And here in Florence what treasures there are : these pic-tures ! these churches ! One would need a whole lifetime to describe them. I especially like the Italians. They are calmly graceful and charming. This will be a great nation, I believe, but very different. A *utilitarian* trend is pervading the world which is trying to make us all alike and perhaps even trying to destroy all national characteristics. Even the ease with which one can travel now is really enough to transform all our living conditions. English society, however, spoils me for all other coun-tries, because the finesse there, the culture of both the head and the heart characteristic of the best English people, are, after all, completely different from the culture of people of other nations. However, the only *nobly spiritual* place is Berlin, at least that's what I believe.

My dear Amalia, how sorry I am that you are still suffering. Oh, how full of sorrows and fears this life is ! And poor *Herr-mann*. Oh, if only he could get well in spite of everything ! Has he ever tried homeopathy ? Perhaps this could help to alleviate the illness, even if he couldn't cure it completely. Give him and his wife my most heartfelt greetings and kiss the children for me, especially my little *Johannes*. I certainly hope that little Cecilia won't ever acquire a *nose* like mine. The two children are much too handsome to resemble me in the slightest, very älskade Fru !

Old *Louise* Johanssen is very ill in Sweden with her husband ! (What a condition !) If they didn't get a small pension from me, the situation of those poor people would be really bad. And good, stupid Louise could certainly have done without *marriage*, believe me !

I probably don't need to tell you, my sweet Amalia, that we are not going to move to Berlin. My husband loves England much too much to want to live anywhere else. Even now he is still very well known and highly esteemed there. I have to go to Cannes during the winter, and I couldn't stand the German climate much better than the English one. Moreover, Otto is not young for his sons. Of course he looks young, but he is beginning to be not quite so agile and vigorous as he was . . . Strange that our old friend Comthur (?) is still so vigorous. I should certainly like to see how he looks now. Oh, Taubert, my good Taubert! Werder, Lenné, Mendelssohn, Rungenhagen, Meyerbeer! You good old Prince Wittgenstein! You beloved old King! My much loved Queen Elizabeth! These are old visions on the proscenium of *my opera-house,* and I still feel their *wit* and genuineness whenever I reminisce in this way about that first evening when I sang *Norma* and when my success was assured after I sang "Casta Diva"! And Taubert's half-friendly, half-formal face in front of me in the orchestra, and that stupid Bredendorff as Adolphina, that dramatically noisy but well-intentioned Birch-Pfeiffer sobbing in front of us with her motherly enthusiasm and simply carried away with delight! Oh, now I am an old woman; I have already travelled quite far along the pathway of life, and I am thinking only of the future of my children, and am full of wonder that I was able to accomplish anything. That is the way life goes. May the benevolent God lead us through this vale of tears to His eternal peace, and may He bless you and yours during this and all coming years! This is the wish, in enduring love, of your true and loving

                    Jenny L. Goldschmidt

Towards the end of the year she sent this letter:

LXXII

                                    Oak Lea, December 6th (1872)
Dear Amalia:

It is two weeks since I received your nice letter of November 12th. How quickly time runs by! Dear Amalia, how faithful you are and how deeply I am moved by your faithfulness. In my own heart everything is, and always will be, the same as in the old days. And I can truly say that I experienced the purest, deepest joy of my whole life with you and yours! It is inexpressibly sad that you are still suffering so much, my dear Amalia. And also poor Herrmann . . . May God guide us to Himself through all these trials; then we shall not have suffered in vain.

I have so much to say, but I should need weeks to do it in. In July and August I was very ill from sunstroke, something approaching both a gastric and a rheumatic fever. Still, I managed to stay alive and I am much stronger, *much* healthier than I have been in the last twenty years! I hardly feel my fifty-two years! My husband is not as energetic as I am. But he is strong. For three months he has suffered from *boils,* which have given him a lot of trouble; so I have often been busy as nurse. He is really so devoted to me, and has such confidence in everything I *permit,* or perchance *forbid,* that every day I am deeply touched. How pure and noble a human being can be whose true art is alive with a deep faith! He constantly reminds me of *that friend* who departed from us on the fourth of November twenty-five years ago![63] Oh, dear Amalia! How full life is with painful—and beautiful—memories!

Since the 10th of August my Jenny has been at school in *Düsseldorf.* The day of our parting was perhaps one of the most difficult of my whole life. Yet things are better this way. She needed other young people; besides, England is dangerous for her at her present age, and the youth of our neighbourhood leaves much to be desired.

Walter is at Oxford at one of the best colleges there. He is unlikely to die from overwork! But he has the power to please people easily, and if he only decides to employ this gift rightly and nobly, then he will certainly become a good person. God in His grace will surely help toward that end.

Ernest is also at a school half-an-hour from here; thus Otto and I are alone together, but we still have so much in common that the day is never long enough for us to complete our mutual exchange of ideas. The *honney-moon* (sic), as the English say, for us anyway, is still in full force!!

But this is really not all I meant to say. You know that in a few days I am going to Düsseldorf to my Jenny so as to spend Christmas with our relatives. If Otto is well enough he will come too, with Walter and Ernest. In any case, I am planning to go to Berlin for a few days so as to present my Jenny to you and to see you and the Herrmanns. I must talk with you about many things, and I simply cannot be so near to Berlin without going

[63] Mendelssohn.

there. Therefore, I hope that I shall be seeing you soon. May God grant that you will not say you are too ill to see me. It will do you good to see my old face once more. I hope to arrive at Jenny's about the 15th or 16th of this month, but a few lines would reach me most safely in Hamburg at this address.

Frau Dr. Felix Goldschmidt, 9 Grosse Theater Strasse, Hamburg.

I did not know that Magnus had died so sadly. Merciful heavens! Herr Berg is still living, and in Stockholm. He is still very active, it appears. His wife died several years ago. His deaf and dumb son has a very nice wife. His daughter, Helene, made a rich marriage twelve years ago, etc.

Now, goodbye, my sweet Amalia. I could chat on in this way for a long time, having got into the mood, but I have really taxed you long enough.

I hope that the Crown Prince of Prussia is well again. Herr Ernest von Bunsen told me recently that the Prince possesses an iron constitution. May his dear life be spared for many, many years!

Sincerest greetings to Clara and Herrmann *and* to my Rudolph. But most of all I send my greetings to you, yourself. From your true-unto-death, loving

Jenny L. Goldschmidt

P.S. Now, really, don't tell me that Herrmann's children promise to become so ugly as to resemble me!

LXXIII

Oak Lea, Wimbledon Park, January 8, 1873

Dear Amalia:

Only yesterday did I receive your generous lines of the 13th December. My little mother-in-law had kept the letter for herself. You will be surprised to see me still *here*. But I couldn't leave. My husband has been plagued with boils for three months, and was so sick (shortly after I wrote to you) that although I had my luggage packed I had to forego the trip; so Walter went to

Düsseldorf and fetched his sister home. *L'homme propose, et Dieu dispose!*

Otto is much better now although not completely recovered yet, and so I hope to take Jenny back to her school within eight to ten days. But now I can't present my daughter to my dear Amalia. How sorry I am to have missed Rudolph and his wife, but that's the way it always is with me (and probably with other people too!). But perhaps it is rather a good thing for you, dear Amalia, that you did not have all of us on a visit, for we might have over-excited you. Yet I still have a deep desire to go to Berlin later, but I cannot definitely fix the time yet. Meanwhile my husband must have a change of climate, and if Ernest and Walter keep healthy (they are both strong, praise the Lord!) then we *old folk* can really go where we want to.

At times I am fairly worn out by this continuous house-keeping and the responsibility for the children's upbringing, and I too need a bit of freedom. Therefore, I hope that my trip to Germany will be of fairly long duration, and then I will come and visit you and tell you *all kinds of things*. I am badly in need of it! So I won't write any more, so as not to strain you overmuch, but I will close my epistle with the heartfelt wish that this New Year will bring joy and blessedness. That your dear life will still be preserved for your children is the prayer of your loving

Jenny L. Goldschmidt

LXXIV

Oak Lea, March 17, Monday (1873)

My dear Amalia:

I was both ashamed and touched when I received your dear, dear letter here. How can I ever thank you for all your kindness and loyalty? I can hardly understand how you find the strength for writing letters!! But you are a pearl! Your rooms with all their furnishings reawakened so many things in my memory.[64] I cannot put into words what I felt when, at the

---

[64] The reference is obviously to pictures which Amalia had sent to Jenny.

sight of all these things, I was so vividly reminded of all we have experienced together! Life, sweet Amalia, is difficult and earnest, and if one has remained as much a *child* as I have, and if one really doesn't understand very well how *to be a support* for others but rather needs a support (spiritual, that is) for oneself— then it is all the better to be back with someone whom one admires as a true *mother,* as I admire you!

You possess that rare peace and that orderly way and manner which we artists lack so completely (with a few exceptions), and for this reason also you are such a mainstay to those close to you. How I hope that you will recover and that God will keep you among us for a long, long time yet. You are my link with Germany, and indeed with the most wonderful years of my life. Dear Amalia, if I dare offer a bit of advice, I should say that you simply ought to move and take up your future residence in Herrmann's house. It would be a great comfort for you all if you were under the same roof. Herrmann will not always be able to go to your house in summer, and Clara cannot always get away from the children; but if you are in the same house, then you will always have Clara and the children with you. And secondary things such as higher rents and lack of exterior elegance (my Amalia knows only too well how to provide for true interior elegance) shouldn't really play an important part if you accept the place with its garden. And truly your present house is by no means worth 2,000 Thaler! Then, too, the evil-smelling waters of the canal harbour area must give out a real perfume in the summer time! This is serious for your throat and your overall state of health. That's my opinion.

My good Professor Werder! Yes, mental illness is the fate of his dear ones. That's the way things go with us human beings in this world, so that we learn to comprehend that our life here is a preparatory existence. Werder seemed not to be at all our old Werder of Potsdam! But Taubert is still a fresh, innocent person. His family life seems very moving to me, and his wife is touching in her simplicity and deep dedication. What is genuine remains genuine, whether it is rich or poor, young or old, beautiful or ugly!

Here at home I found everything fine and in order. I have faithful old servants. My garden is beginning to bloom and the

birds are singing quite charmingly. (I don't know any country
where the birds sing as beautifully as they do in England.)

My dear little Ernest came home on Saturday. (We had
arrived on Thursday.) He went back to school this morning at
8.15. He's a sweet child. I found Jenny very well and happy to
see us. We had the most beautiful spring weather on that Sunday
in Düsseldorf. Now she will stay on until about the end of May,
when she will be fetched for a brief time to celebrate her con-
firmation here in our Church. After that she will probably go
back to Düsseldorf for a little while. Walter is well and will be
coming home soon for his Easter vacation.

My husband asked me to send you his very best greetings. He
esteems you very highly, and, although he appears to be very
quiet and says little, still he has a deep affection for you, and he
is happy for *me* that I still possess you as my friend.

A thousand thanks for your *dear* letter. May God bless and
protect you and yours. Many affectionate greetings to Clara
and Herrmann from the two of us, and so farewell for this time,
dear Amalia. As long as I live, I shall feel the same affection for
you and I remain always, in faithful love,

Your devoted
Jenny L. Goldschmidt

The Goldschmidts and their three children had a full life
during this period of their lives. They often went to Scotland and
the Lakes, to Sweden, and to Europe. Jenny also went to Wiesbaden, as she found the waters helpful for her rheumatism.
Because of the English climate she had taken to wearing the fine
Indian shawls which became familiar articles of her dress : two
of them had been given to her by Queen Victoria.

The children were growing up, and the Goldschmidts were
taking an active part in the social and musical life of London.
Jenny used to enjoy taking her daughter to the opera house,
where the seats only cost 4/- or so. Reluctantly, they decided
they must live nearer to the centre of the town, so they sold the
house in Wimbledon and rented a furnished house in Barnes
before buying one in South Kensington.

Here is a letter written from Wiesbaden :

LXXV

Wiesbaden, February 12, 1874

Dear Amalia:

How long it has been my wish to write to you, and how thankful I am for your lines of the 16th January, I can only explain that my life is always very busy. I am the focal point of my family, and I have no one who will act as a substitute! And so I can't always find the time to write to my dearest friends.

My Amalia, once again you have been sick for so long a time. What a patient sufferer you are. I believe that it is your *courage* alone that keeps you alive. In the hereafter you will find peace, my dear. This life is after all only a sad tale of suffering.

I do not see as much of Frau Dr. Kunde and Frau von Lepel as I should like to. Unfortunately, both these ladies are so often ill, and when I call on them they are either sick or not at home. On the other hand, when the kind Frau Doctor comes to see me then I am out! In this way we always miss each other, and she simply never lets me know when she is coming. Poor creature! She pays me such exaggerated compliments that my mind ceases to function and I cannot find an answer to them. It is really a pity. She is so good and kind-hearted, except that she is much too formal. Sweet Anina becomes quite lively whenever Papa comes. The Major is pleasant and has elegant manners, and loves Italy. But Frau von Lepel is very often quite ill, much more than I am. I believe the climate of Wiesbaden does not suit her. I myself have been very well here. For example, I haven't even felt my throat here, which is a great boon for me.

My husband and Jenny are in Hamburg at the moment. Walter is at Oxford and Ernest is at his school in the neighbourhood of *Oak Lea*. In the middle of March we shall leave here. I shall go straight home. My husband must drink the waters at Weilbach, and therefore he will probably stay in Germany until June.

I am so sorry that you are not satisfied with your new apartment. The situation seemed so good to me. Of course, things were very nice back at Hafenplatz. Our children, you know, will keep us tied down to England for some time. Otherwise I should have liked to move here, since my health is so completely different here from what it was in the terrible English climate.

And especially now that our financial means are really quite insufficient there. Oh, what sacrifices one makes for one's children! A parent's whole life is one long, unceasing sacrifice.

May God be with you, dear Amalia. I am and shall always be devoted to you with deepest love.

Your
Jenny L. Goldschmidt
(P.S.) Most cordial greetings to Herrmann and Clara.

Later that year Jenny despatched a note to Amalia:

LXXVI

Brighton, October 28, 1874
My beloved Amalia:

May I ask you for the great favour of kindly forwarding the enclosed letter to dear Frau Louise von Illaire at Sanscouci (sic)? Also please write the address on it, since I don't know whether or not she should be addressed with the title "Excellency" and I don't want to send it with a stupid address. She is living in Sanscouci in the house which the gracious King gave her husband. I have owed the dear woman this letter for a year, and I only pray to the Lord that she will still be alive.

I hope that you have received my last letter? Forgive me, my dear Amalia, my address for this winter is

11 Cleveland Road
Barnes London S W

How are you these days, my dear?

Your deeply loving
Jenny L. Goldschmidt

Thus ends the correspondence which Jenny so faithfully maintained with the woman whom she admired perhaps more than any other. Amalia Wichmann must have died in the year 1876, for there is the following reference on page 363 of the first volume of Holland and Rockstro: "The original picture [Magnus's painting of Jenny Lind] remained in the Wichmann family until the year 1877, when the Professor's eldest son, Herr

Herrmann Wichmann, to whom it had passed by inheritance after his mother's death *in the previous year* [our italics], consented to its removal, at the price of twelve thousand thalers, to the Berlin National Gallery . . . "

Before drawing the final curtain on the Goldschmidts, let us take a brief look at their subsequent years together.

Sir William Sterndale Bennett, who had been a great friend and ally of Otto Goldschmidt, died on February 1, 1875, and was buried in Westminster Abbey. Because of his death, Otto Goldschmidt retired from active service at the Royal Academy, although he did remain on the governing body. He was, too, a member of the Royal College of Organists, the Royal College of Music, the Swedish Royal Academy of Music and the London Company of Musicians. He took a real part in musical education in England, and was a valued authority, consulted freely by fellow musicians during his twenty years of life following Jenny's death in 1887. Then, too, he was an enthusiastic member of the Madrigal Society long before the greatest and last musical interest in his life, the Bach Choir.

A small private choir of twenty-two voices, the best amateurs of the day, had been meeting once a week at the Goldschmidts' house to sing *a capella* works by Palestrina, Orlando Lasso, Purcell, Weelkes, etc., as well as Bach motets. Through the tenor Arthur Coleridge they became interested in Bach's B Minor Mass —which was then totally unknown in England—and decided to present the first performance in this country under Otto Goldschmidt's conductorship. Soon the choir outgrew the Goldschmidts' house, and they transferred their meetings, first to the home of friends who lived at Cromwell House, and later to the lecture room of the South Kensington Museum. On November 19, 1875, sixty-five amateurs attended the first rehearsal. Jenny Goldschmidt led the soprano, and coached the ladies at her own home. The mass was performed in its entirety at St. James's Hall on April 26, 1876, and the Bach Choir had established its place in the musical history of London.

Many years before, during her single years, Jenny Lind Goldschmidt had complained of her loneliness and her dislike of the business details with which she had to cope. Her husband, from the moment of their marriage, protected her from all these matters, and looked after her in every way that was in his power during the concert tours which they made together during fifteen years of their married life.

No. 1, Moreton Gardens, South Kensington, their last London home, became a well-known address during the latter years of the lives of Otto and Jenny Goldschmidt. One may find little formal notes written in Jenny's hand with this address at the top. The ground floor rooms adapted themselves to parties and dances for the growing Goldschmidt children, and many of the young men who had been invited to dance sought a few turns with Jenny. She continued to sing for benefits or special funds, following her lifetime trend of donating her talents to assist her fellow man. Jenny Maude believed that her mother maintained the quality and timbre of her voice to the very end, although some of the critics sympathetically demurred on this point.

The last time that she sang in public was in the year 1883. Five years earlier her daughter had married, and Jenny used often to stay with the Maudes in Herefordshire. She grew to love the surrounding countryside, and bought Wynd's Point, a beautiful house in the Malvern Hills, which today belongs to the Cadbury family, and is still furnished exactly as it was when she was living there. There the Goldschmidts used to spend the summer months. One day the porter who handled the train baggage calmly asked her if she would sing at the annual Railwaymen's Benefit Concert. She was so amused and taken by surprise that she consented. Needless to say, there was an overflowing audience.

In the garden of Wynd's Point she planted a myrtle which had originally come from a sprig that had been in her bridal bouquet. (The myrtle is the national flower of Sweden, and can be seen in the beautiful portrait of Jenny Lind by Sodermark which is now in the possession of her great granddaughter, Mrs. Woods.) Since then a sprig of myrtle has always been part of the wedding bouquets of her descendants—either from the plant at Wynd's Point or from shrubs propagated from it by her grandson, Cyril Maude.

In 1883, at the request of the Prince of Wales, she accepted the post of first Professor of Singing in the Royal College of Music, then being inaugurated in South Kensington with Sir George Grove as Principal. Since the College had no adequate building, the fortunate pupils attended classes in Jenny's own large drawing-room at Moreton Gardens.

She had very definite ideas about the training of a singer. These she embodied in a memorandum, as well as writing at length about them to the Director of the Musical Conservatory in Stockholm. Though her standards were extremely high, and some of her pupils were rather overwhelmed, they found her a wonderful and inspiring teacher.

This teaching was continued for three years and then given up because of a lack of physical strength and an increasing awareness of a debilitating illness. Summers were still spent in Malvern, and the last winter of her life found her once again at Cannes. Otto was not with her, for he had engagements in London. Early in the new year, a letter reached him from her doctor announcing that she had cancer. Immediately he hurried to Cannes, and stayed with her there for some months. When they returned to England in May Jenny seemed somewhat better, but gradually she grew weaker, and on November 2 she died. That morning, as her daughter drew back the curtains and let in the sunshine, her lips formed the opening bars of Schumann's *An den Sonnenschein*.

Jenny Lind's memorial in Westminster Abbey, placed in Poets' Corner beneath Handel's, will always be a spot sacred to music lovers. For here is commemorated what may well be the greatest voice the world has ever heard.

As this little volume proves, Jenny was not only a great singer, but a true and loving friend. These letters, spanning nearly all the years of a fame which inspired an affection that has been felt for few public figures before or since, reveal her faithfulness, humility and never-failing helpfulness towards her correspondent. There was never a shadow cast over this loyal friendship of more than three decades.

APPENDIX

I   H.R., Vol. I, p. 299. The original of this letter is not in our collection, and we quote it verbatim from Holland and Rockstro.

II   H.R., Vol. I, p. 349.

III   H.R., Vol. I, p. 373. Only the second and third paragraphs were quoted in Holland and Rockstro, and the sentence which begins "I am staying with the Brockhauses".

IV   H.R., Vol. I, p. 395. Holland and Rockstro quoted only the third, fourth and seventh paragraphs.

V   H.R., Vol. I, p. 395. Holland and Rockstro omitted the first and fourth paragraphs, most of the twelfth paragraph, and the brief one beginning 'With divine weapons'.

VI   H.R., Vol. I, p. 415. This letter is not a part of our collection, and apparently was never kept with it in the past, for Rudolph Wichmann placed it by itself in the hands of Otto Goldschmidt in about the year 1888 for its use in the biography.

VII   H.R., Vol. I, p. 421. This letter, and the two which follow, are rare instances of letters to Amalia which do not form part of our collection.

VIII   H.R., Vol. I, p. 424.

IX   H.R., Vol. I, p. 426.

X   This letter was not used by Holland and Rockstro. It was hastily penned, and proved rather difficult to decipher.

XI   H.R., Vol. II, p. 333. This letter is not in our collection.

XII   H.R., Vol. II, p. 6. Holland and Rockstro omitted the whole of the first paragraph except the opening sentence, the second, third, sixth and last paragraphs, and the postscript.

XIII   H.R., Vol. II, p. 19. Holland and Rockstro print only the first two and the last three paragraphs, and the first postscript.

XIV   This letter does not appear in Holland and Rockstro.

XV   H.R., Vol. II, p. 39. This letter is not in our collection.

XVI   H.R., Vol. II, p. 40. The sixth and eighth paragraphs are omitted in Holland and Rockstro, as well as the second sentence of the letter.

XVII   H.R., Vol. II. This letter is not part of our collection. It is separated and printed in two portions in Holland and Rockstro, the first two paragraphs appearing on page 181 and the last paragraph on page 188.

XVIII H.R., Vol. II, p. 182. Holland and Rockstro quoted only the third and fourth paragraphs and the postscript.

XIX   H.R., Vol. II. This letter was split in two, for purposes of reference, in Holland and Rockstro. The first paragraph appears on page 335 and the second on page 181.

XX   H.R., Vol. II, p. 183.

XXI   H.R., Vol. II, p. 191 and p. 193. Holland and Rockstro used of this letter only the passage "I am so happy . . . they love me for that" and the sentence beginning "I have no fear".

XXII   This letter does not appear in Holland and Rockstro.

XXIII H.R., Vol. II, p. 338. This letter is not in our collection.

XXIV   This letter does not appear in Holland and Rockstro.

XXV H.R., Vol. II, p. 217. Holland and Rockstro quoted only the last two sentences of the fourth paragraph, and the penultimate paragraph.

XXVI H.R., Vol. II, p. 237. Holland and Rockstro printed most of this letter, omitting only the second paragraph and a word or two here and there.

XXVII H.R., Vol. II, pp. 350/1. Not in our collection.

XXVIII Holland and Rockstro made no mention of this letter.

XXIX H.R., Vol. II, pp. 350/1. Not in our collection. collection.

XXX H.R., Vol. II, p. 356. This letter is not in our collection, and unfortunately seems not to have been reproduced in its entirety. Nor is any date given.

XXXI H.R., Vol. II, p. 360. This letter is not in our collection.

XXXII H.R., Vol. II, pp. 371/2. This letter is not in our collection. Holland and Rockstro unfortunately omitted the first page, which they described as "entirely personal".

XXXIII H.R., Vol. II, p. 380. Holland and Rockstro did not print the first, second and last paragraphs, and they also omitted two or three phrases.

XXXIV H.R., Vol. II, p. 380. Holland and Rockstro omitted the penultimate paragraph.

XXXV H.R., Vol. II, p. 393. This letter is not in our collection, and is only reproduced in part in Holland and Rockstro.

XXXVI Holland and Rockstro referred briefly to this letter but did not actually quote any part of it.

XXXVII H.R., Vol. II, p. 422. This is the last letter to Amalia Wichmann which Holland and Rockstro quoted. They printed most of it, omitting sentences and phrases here and there.